ODES TO TOADS

Bridget Alberts

ATHENA PRESS
LONDON

First Published 2002 by
ATHENA PRESS
Queen's House, 2 Holly Road
Twickenham TW1 4EG
United Kingdom

Printed for Athena Press

ODES TO TOADS

*To Tessa and Simon
from Mummy and Daddy
with love.*

December 2001

Richard and I at Princes

Odes to Toads

Toads are extraordinarily loveable animals. Superstition and prejudice have brought them much persecution over the centuries. The most comical in temperament and the most loveable toad is the Natterjack Toad. It has a lively comical movement because the hind legs are relatively short, consequently this toad runs more than it hops. The most common European toad is the Common Toad. Most specimens are an inconspicuous olive-green or brown, but attractive rust-red tinted animals also occur. Newly transformed toadlets of the rust-red colour are comical handsome fellows. The European Common Toad Bufo has figured greatly in literature and legend.[1]

Ode to India

Bombay harbour looks like a huge diamond necklace beckoning the weary traveller to return to India one day. But how can one achieve this dream? All dreams can come true but it takes a lot of hard work to make one dream come true. As the ship sailed away from the land of my birth leaving my beloved parents behind my tears flowed like the Bramaputra, the Hooghly, the Ganges and the Nerbudda.

But today I feel that 'I've got the world on a string' like the song because I have finished my *Odes to Toads*.

---

[1] Johann Krottlinger, *Keeping Reptiles and Amphibians.*

Ode to my First Poem

When I'm a grown up lady
I'll have a silver purse.
I'll have a little baby girl
And she shall have a nurse.

I do not remember the rest. Ironically I did have a little baby girl
and a little baby boy and they had ayahs when I lived in India.

Ode to Cesar

I thought I was a lighthouse
But I'm being dashed into the sea
Oh Cesar! Please Cesar!
Come and rescue me
The night is so dark
There's no moon in the sky
I taught you how to live once
Please teach me how to die.

Ode to Snow-Boy
My Faithful Poodle

My dearest darling Snow-Boy
You're the best friend I've ever had
Because you seem to know when I'm sad
When I feel flirtatious and wink
You look back at me and blink
When I'm gay you dance with me too
But when I'm sad you also feel blue
When I'm ill you lie beneath my bed
We'll remain good friends until we're dead.

Ode to the Menopause

Menopause, there's no such word
It should be pause-o-not from men
Women should keep their femininity forever
Keep men on a lead!

Ode to the great G S

When the great GS begins to pull the strings
All his little puppets begin to do things
Some like to dance, some like to sing
But poor old *My Fair Lady*
Only wants to swing!

Ode to baby-sitting

I enjoyed baby-sitting again last night for Sophie, Lucy, Kate and
Emma. I taught Sophie and Lucy the tongue twister that I learnt
when I was a tiny 'blue-bird' many years ago. I still remember this
funny little ditty which goes like this:

> Chicker racka chee chi cho chicka lorum
> Koda lorum one pack one
> Oko oko iki acki oh
> Kiterpi iterpie chee chi cho.

Sophie at ten years old has a natural gift of mastering the English
language, her diction is perfect, but little Lucy who is six had a
struggle; however, at the end of an enchanting evening both girls
knew the complicated song 'pit-pat'. My grandchildren are very
talented and baby-sitting is becoming a very rewarding
occupation.

Ode to Mother's Day

Mother's Day was the loveliest Sunday! My son Simon and his wife Susie had invited my husband Richard and I for lunch. We had pink champagne and caviar on arrival followed by an excellent meal of roast beef with all the trimmings, and delicious profiteroles with chocolate sauce and cream for desert. My granddaughter Jessica was dressed in a gorgeous red velvet dress looking every inch like Scarlett O'Hara at the age of two! Her brothers, Oliver eight, and Dominic five, were smartly turned out and they behaved impeccably. I had great fun after lunch dancing for handsome Dominic to 'Bomboleo' a fantastic tune by the Gypsy Kings. Dominic was very amused, he pulled his coat over his head pretending to be shy of his crazy grandmother's antics but he was secretly peeping through a button hole in his jacket. Dominic is exactly like his father was when he was a child, he appears to be a little boy lost with his head in the clouds but he is full of mischief. Simon gave me an exquisite Leedsware Pottery Plate, it must have cost a bomb. The pink champagne and excellent fruity red wine went straight to my head and I made a hasty departure from 'Hartfield' in a disorderly fashion leaving my amusing Mother's Day card behind.

I called in at 'Weybourne' later and I found my poor daughter Tessa in utter chaos. What an awful Mother's Day she must have had. She's had builders and decorators in for weeks. Her harassed 'do-it-yourself' husband was busy frantically using his electric drill moving light points on the lounge ceiling. The entire house was upside down. But in spite of all the confusion she presented me with a lovely pot of red azaleas and an amusing card. I was distressed to see her in such a turmoil especially as I had had a wonderful Mother's Day.

Ode to a Cheetah and a Fox

A cheetah is the fastest animal on earth; it relies on its speed to catch its prey but unfortunately it can only run short distances. It selects an animal from a herd, creeping up as close as possible, then it suddenly sprints forward at lightning speed. The frightened herd scatters but the cheetah pursues its victim. It is very important for this magnificent animal to keep up with its prey for the first few hundred yards because it is unable to run at great speeds for long. The hunt ends dramatically when the cheetah bites the throat of its victim in order to kill it. This chase is a fair one because the cheetah only hunts when hungry in order to survive in its own territory in Asia.

However, the fox is found in all parts of the world and this cunning animal is able to survive anywhere, even in a burning desert. I would hate to be a fennec fox, its giant ears work rather like radiators. They give off heat to help keep the fox cool. They also enable it to detect sounds made by the small birds and animals it hunts when it emerges from its burrow at dusk. My favourite fox is the red fox because it is both secretive and intelligent. This animal normally hunts by night preying on birds and small mammals. The vixen takes her cubs on nightly expeditions in order to teach them to hunt. Foxes can change their diet and habits and they now hunt in gardens and parks because they can adapt to city life where there is plenty of space and shelter and food is easy to find.

A cheetah is not a clever hunter, one has to be as cunning as a fox in order not to fall into too many booby traps! 'Born Free' is playing on the radio and I must bring this ode to an end because my daughter wants me to pick up Kate. When I arrived at 'Weybourne' both Kate and little Emma were screeching their heads off. The decorators were all over the place and since Kate is not well I will bring her back with me for some peace and quite.

Ode to School Runs

I had a private ego trip today when I drove to Woburn Hill in order to collect my Mother's Day card from Oliver. As I drove up the long drive I began to remember many happy memories of when I was a young mother. I had a splendid tobacco coloured Rover in those days which my wonderful son kept like a Rolls Royce. The senior boys still looked the same but I no longer had young admirers waiting to get a glimpse of me. I remember one boy in particular called Anthony caught my roving eye on many occasions, he, like my son, was always so smartly turned out because he had a caring mother. Poor Anthony, like many young men I had met during the war, crashed his plane when his father was giving him a flying lesson on Easter Sunday. What a terrible tragedy! His grieving mother who was a great friend of mine never got over this ghastly accident. She knew that I liked Anthony and she thoroughly approved of it because she liked my son. To ease her pain and mine I quickly bought a red leather frame and I placed handsome Anthony lovingly in it so that we could both remember him forever. This courageous lady has since died but we remained good friends as long as she lived in Weybridge. Ironically Easter is just around the corner and I like to think that Anthony and his loving mother are both helping me to launch my musical odes.

Anthony was only seventeen when he blew himself up and I like to think that I made him happy during the awkward adolescent years from boyhood to manhood. Those precious years when children need encouragement and understanding and foolish mothers can either make or break a character for life.

I was actually helping three teenagers who turned to me for support, one was my son Simon, and a Spanish student called Cesar who was rebelling against his destiny. He was a rich banker's son with the soul of an artist. I called him my 'summer love' but I turned to Anthony for comfort and understanding in winter and I asked him to read my book *The Summer of our Love*, which he enjoyed. It was about the Oedipus complex many women and men go through. I can still remember a happy Sports Day when Simon was sixteen and he was shouted down by a curious gang of boys, 'Hi, Simon, is that your mother or your sister?'

And Simon who was tickled pink walked proudly beside me. I no longer go to exciting Sports Days but I often pick up my two handsome young grandsons from Woburn Hill and take them out to tea. Tessa's son James is eleven and Simon's son Oliver is eight. Children either have or have not got style and yesterday when I called to collect my Mother's Day card from Oliver my two grandsons had unmistakable style, the other little boys by comparison looked like a bunch of ragamuffins! James tuned my car radio to BBC2 for me because I enjoy music and suddenly Oliver appeared like a smart young executive with his satchel and he delivered my important Mother's Day card with great panache! James and I met up again on my way home, he was riding his new racing bike and I was driving my new UNO. Every time I thought I had lost him he would catch up again when I was trapped in a traffic jam.

'Where's Ollie?' he asked as he scooted past.

'He's gone home with his au pair,' I shouted. I playfully tooted him several times en route and when we eventually parted I waved my Mother's Day card from Simon which I had collected from Oliver like a teenager in love!

It is a glorious spring day today but I am absolutely exhausted after looking after Kate for a day, children are very demanding little people. How does my wonderful daughter cope with her 'infamous five'? Tessa dropped in with Lucy and Emma for lunch and she will be taking Kate home with her. I am baby-sitting again tonight. At the moment Alison Moyet is belting out one of my favourite songs, 'The old devil called love' but I refuse to be lured into the tender trap again.

I'm afraid the ideal man in my life has to be a father, a brother, a lover, a son and above all a kind understanding friend!

Ode to James

My grandson James brought me up to date in my musical taste. He first put in a video of Tina Turner because he likes some of the songs she sings, although we both agreed that the lady did not have style – but I am also a Tina Turner fan. She definitely has animal magic which is important in show business!

As the night progressed I was fascinated by a tape called 'Italia dance music from Italy'. The rhythm was fantastic and I wanted to escape with James to Amalfi to a night club called 'The Africana'. I first got the idea to become a writer in Positano in Italy when I took a course of oestrogen.

The evening ended romantically with Elvis singing 'Only make believe', darling James had carefully copied down all the romantic words. I have met the pretty girl he likes, she is one of my granddaughter Sophie's friends. Could James be falling in love at the age of eleven? I'm quite certain he is if he is anything like his romantic grandmother. I adore children, especially my own grandchildren because they are all in love with life!

My daughter Tessa is coming over for lunch again because the decorators will be working in her kitchen today. I must end this ode now with one of James Last's records. He was Gloria Hunniford's guest this afternoon, he ended his interview with very wise words:

'Good music is like good medicine.'

Ode to a Garden

The Secret Garden was an enchanting film especially as it concerned what a couple of children achieved when they made a derelict garden come to life again. When one comes to think of it God created Adam and Eve in a garden, and it is a great pity that man has exploited his environment as it would be a wonderful world if we built our lives around one big garden and enjoyed ourselves. I presume that it is impossible to visualise what life would be like without man's mechanical inventions. For instance, there would be no motor cars, aeroplanes or ships, and above all no motorways and traffic jams.

I would like to live in an ideal world where everything stays the same because it would indeed be a peaceful one. Imagine getting up every morning to the dawn chorus of birds instead of the noise of traffic? Every season will paint a new picture for us to view. Nature awakens in spring, blooms in summer and in autumn she covers everything carefully with a beautiful blanket of multicoloured autumn leaves. Even winter adorns the garden with a sprinkling of frost or snow in order to keep the grass alive until the following spring.

I wish all God's creatures could live in a garden of Eden here on earth in perfect harmony in the garden of *love*!

Ode to Happiness

What is happiness? Is it a fleeting moment or can it be achieved for a lifetime? Everyone is an individual so what makes one person happy does not necessarily make another. Some people strive for worldly possessions – success, money, and the good life whilst others are content to take each day as it comes and thank God that they are alive. I think that it is very important to be a happy person because one can make other people happy as well. To be born with a happy character must be one of the greatest gifts, far better than being born rich! It is quite wrong to think that money and happiness go together because very often money can actually buy unhappiness. For instance, some people spend far too much time trying to earn a lot of money for their families and they often end up with nothing because they have accidentally neglected their emotional needs. One thing is very clear that money can buy material needs but it cannot buy *love*!

It would be nice to have a happy and contented environment but unfortunately human beings and animals always fail to see that they can live happily with one another. If only we can try to remember the proverb: United we stand, divided we fall'. What is this kind of madness that seems to come over us which makes us fight for our own survival? Surely we must all sink or swim together and when the race of life is over we can all come out as winners! There should be no losers because in my opinion life's a game and very often one has to lose in order to win!

Ode to Never Judge a Book by its Cover

How can one judge a book by its cover or a famous painting like the *Mona Lisa* by her smile? I have to admit that I always fell into a trap when I was young by judging people by their 'masks' instead of trying to read them like a book. We all have human failings and for some of us life has been an obstacle race and we want to leave a few words of advice for our children but it is a vain pursuit because children, like us, have to learn from their own experiences.

I sometimes look back on my life with deep regret because of the mistakes I have made but now I am an 'open book' for all to read, nothing is secret or sacred anymore. Many times people do judge one another wrongly at first and the damage can last a lifetime.

In my opinion only God has the right to pass the final judgement on us and I am sure that He will forgive all of us in the end, remember:

To err is human, to forgive divine.

Ode to Police Talk

I thought that all police cars were equipped with intercoms and telephones in order to carry out their duties without holding up the congested traffic in Weybridge.

However, as I drove down a side road to get to Waitrose I came across two police cars which were blocking the road and the occupants were having a chat from one car to the other. I carried on driving carefully in order not to cause a traffic jam and as I caught the young PC's eyes I said, 'No talking.'

It was just a playful incident but one police car followed me and made me pull over into a road on the left, and made me stop on the double yellow lines. Again I tried to humour these angry men by pointing to the double yellow lines, telling them that I would park on the right hand side of the road which had no yellow lines. Out came the young bullies all geared up to prove their point.

'We are chasing some robbers who are in this district,' they told me. I wonder what would happen if all law abiding citizens stopped their cars in the middle of the road in order to discuss their business!

'I thought the British police had the best sense of humour in the world!' I told them politely. 'Do you want to take this matter further?' I asked, referring to them by their numbers which I could see clearly without any spectacles.

'No,' was their prompt reply when I showed them I had a writing pad in my car.

It felt good to be involved in 'Police Talk' especially when the boot was on the other foot! I think that this incident would make interesting reading. Any offers? A seventy-one-year-old OAP.

Ode to the Importance of Work

People who work in the community lead very interesting lives. There are too many hours in the day, too many days in the week and too many weeks in the year to live in solitude doing nothing but housework. Human beings have a lot to learn from the animals and insects who share our planet with us. For instance the leaf cutter ants in America all work together and they have become a very successful colony. Bees are also social insects and it is interesting to learn that the first job a bee does is housekeeping!

Animals, like human beings also want to be clean and healthy to survive, and many animals including birds constantly groom themselves and one another. Ironically the 'vulture' is one of the cleanest birds! Some animals like buffaloes have to depend on birds to do the difficult jobs for them. Ants are very tidy and clean and because they are highly organised no job is too big for them. Some birds like the screech owls have messy nests but by sheer accident blind snakes enter their homes and clean them up! In the same way human beings resort to mechanical gadgets to help them with their work but the human body must be fit and strong or we will all land up in old people's homes!

I have seen a programme on TV today about the busy life of a seventy-eight-year-old widow who runs a pub working very long hours. I would be bored working in a pub seeing the same old faces calling in for their pints of beer. I work in my own home taking in lodgers. I am a lonely 'swallow' who is trying desperately hard to fly into the community to find friends. I am tired of being treated like a 'buffoon' with loud noises in my head.

Ode to Dishcloths

If dishcloths could talk they would tell many absorbing stories. For instance a quarrel at the sink: 'It's your turn to dry up.'

Never throw an old dishcloth away. I have been keeping my dishcloths since 1986, they have all been washed and ironed and carefully stored. I am a widow now so I buy amusing dishcloths to keep me cheerful in my kitchen. I went on a shopping spree the other day and I bought ten new dishcloths; six of them are exactly the same. I love Irish linen dishcloths and since I could not resist the clever words of 'The indispensable man' I bought six. Why did I do such a silly irresponsible thing? I am an elderly OAP who has been tied to the kitchen sink for forty-one years and suddenly at the age of seventy-one I want to take up a 'hobby' of writing again. I have been playing 'a cat and mouse' game with psychiatrists for the last nine years. They are a clever pack of foxes who want me to use my brain. They know that I am a lonely Cheetah who is too old to hunt anymore. How has this twenty-year bond with psychiatrists stood the test of *time* which is so important? The reason is simple. Foxes, unlike Cheetahs are very cunning and they have become so bold that they now raid people's dustbins by night. Cheetahs like venison and they hunt by day when they are hungry. The hunt is a good clean chase – survival of the fastest. Foxes and Cheetahs are vastly different animals but ironically they are both endangered species. My clever foxes, who are psychiatrists, have given me back my creative brain so I have decided to use it for my own enjoyment. At last the penny has dropped. Writing is the only true companion I have left apart from my dishcloths!

Ode to Mothers

All mothers are like precious jewels
that can never be replaced!

Ode to Women

Women are like flowers
They need constant love and attention
If you want them to bloom forever!

Ode to Old Age

There are too many hours in the day
Too many days in the week
Too many weeks in the year
And I have lived too long

Ode to Wealth

To be born rich is to be born poor
Because people do not use their natural
talents.

Ode to Religion

The Catholic Church believes –
'Give me a child till seven
And I will show you the man'
I thank God I'm a woman!

Ode to Love

What is love?
It is *loyalty*

Ode to Divorce

It takes two to tango
Two to divorce
But it takes more than two to love
It takes three or four or maybe more
It takes time!

Ode to a Good Motto

United we stand
Divided we fall.

Ode to my Life

My life has been a pack of cards
My romantic 'heart'
Put me in the 'club'
I came to England and
Worked like a 'spade'
Now I want to be a 'diamond'
And sparkle forever!
Words are like diamonds
Shall I continue to write
That is the question?

Ode to a Flasher

I was seventeen years old returning home from Commercial school when a middle-aged Anglo-Indian man enticed me with what I thought was a stick of barley sugar. We were both travelling in a tram in Calcutta. He secretly showed me his penis from under his solar toupee and I foolishly thought that he was offering me barley sugar.

'No thank you,' I replied. 'I am not a child.'

Suddenly it dawned on me what it was, I rushed to the exit and jumped off the tram. Fortunately the tram had just begun to move. I foolishly jumped backwards missing the tram by inches.

This nasty encounter with a wicked man put me off sex for life, previously I had had an enchanting awakening to my power over men!

Ode to Peter

Peter's busy mother was a hard-working physiotherapist so she did not have the time to take four-year-old Peter to the park. I was sixteen years old at the time having just returned from St Joseph's Convent in Kalimpong for the Christmas holidays. I was living with rich Aunt Violet in 19, Theatre Road, Calcutta where she had a nice apartment. Peter's mother lived on the ground floor so she was able to see me roller-skating up and down the long paved drive. This daily activity drew her attention to me.

'I haven't got the time to take Peter to the park,' she told me sadly one day and I was only too happy to be useful.

'I'll take Peter to the park every morning,' I told her, but this job lasted for only two days! The first day Peter reluctantly played on the see-saws and swings. But the second day he complained that he was tired preferring to sit on the park bench with me, and this is when he made a pass at me. Peter moved himself closer and closer and he finally plucked up the courage to put his naughty hands on my tiny rose-bud breasts and this simple act gave him an immediate erection.

I became 'bewitched, bothered and bewildered' like the song so I grabbed hold of his hand and I marched him home.

'Do you want to spend a penny?' I asked him anxiously.

'No! No!' he screamed holding on to his penis.

'I want to marry you when I'm a big man,' he shouted in frustration all the way home.

When we arrived back I promptly handed Peter back to his mother and I told her what had happened. I can still remember how amused she was! I also could not hide my excitement because at sixteen I had had my first proposal of marriage from a little man of four! In spite of the fact that Peter was twelve years younger than me he knew more about life than I did.

That evening as I lay back in my bath I got the first glimpse of my naked body in the chromium taps which drew my attention to the fact that mother nature was decorating my body like a Christmas tree! I was sparkling from head to toe. In boarding school convents in India girls had to wear bathing wrappers so that we would not be tempted to sin. After my bath I rubbed myself down briskly with a large towel then I threw it off and dared to stare at my image in the mirror. I was very curious to know why Peter got an erection when he touched my breasts. It was the mirror on the wall which almost tempted me to find out. I wanted to explore my body so I placed one hand on my breast and the other hand automatically wandered down towards the unknown. My conscience made me withdraw it immediately.

It's a *sin* to touch yourself, I thought. I will go to hell! Hell! Hell!

I am very afraid of hell because when I was a child in the kindergarten we were shown terrible pictures of devils with horns poking the fire, there were all sorts of weird snakes etc., which were plunged into this burning pit along with terrified human beings. The thought of being thrown into hell soon put an end to this natural awakening of my sexuality. I hastily put my clothes on and I forgot all about this incident for years but I was awakened again when I fell in love with a young Canadian fighter pilot during the war. I shall never forget Peter because he was only an innocent child. In a strange way he was my first physical encounter with the opposite sex but definitely not my last!

Hell is no longer horrible pictures, it is here on earth. I have had to cope with a burning sensation like bee stings all over my body, depression and very loud ringing noises in my head for twelve years. Growing old is the worst illness a human being has to endure. I can put up with the physical suffering but tinnitus is like having cancer of the brain because there is no cure for it. It is very difficult to live with loud noises in my head day in and day out. Sleeping pills can block out the noise for a short period but some nights they do not work. I have been told by a clever psychiatrist who channelled my creative brain with an antidepressant that it is in my best interests to write. I have written for psychiatrists for many years, but now I want to write for people who are battling like myself with an incurable illness. I like writing because I have had a very colourful life. It may appear to be a comedy of errors but I would not change it for all the tea in China!

Ode to Christmas

The music was very loud and the rhythm was fantastic! My teenage grandchildren had filled the beautiful house with their kind of music.

I had had an excellent Christmas lunch with all the trimmings at my daughter's house, we had listened to the Queen's speech but now it was time to dance! My family all know that I love music and dancing and I delighted everyone when I began to swing to 'You sexy thing'. I would have preferred to dance with my daughter's father-in-law who is a superb dancer and golfer in spite of his bad arthritis. Many elderly people love music and dancing and I am one of them. I can dance as well as any teenager, in fact far better than them because I have danced from eleven months old! God has many mansions in heaven and I hope He puts me in the ballroom with all the big wartime bands! Sadly Christmas has come and gone but we still have 1998 to look forward to. My daughter gave me very beautiful words the other day which said:

> The past is history,
> The future a mystery,
> But today is a gift
> Which is why we call
> it the present!

I must try to take one day at a time. At the age of seventy-four. Who can ask for anything more?

Ode to the Tango

It is already 28 December and tonight I enjoyed Clive James's fascinating programme on his visit to Buenos Aires especially when he described the tango. I love South American music and dancing and I agree with him that the tango is a very sensual dance.

It was interesting to learn that Latin men must be in full command of this seductive dance because they touch a woman's whole body and yet they are in control of their emotions.

The tango is a dance where pain and passion are acted out on the dance floor but the woman plays a very important part because she controls the man's soul! I wish I could find a soulmate to dance away the lonely hours but I have found that at seventy-four men still want something more!

Ode to Falling in Love

Why do people fall madly in love? Since we all do it we must all be mad! I love being in love because the world changes from grey to bright red! I smile at people and they smile back. I talk to a stranger and he or she talks back. I go around in circles contacting all my friends sharing a few intimate secrets. Personally I fall in love regularly with many people at the same time! It is great fun getting a school girl crush on men because at seventy-four I play the tune! It is the chase not the kill in the mating game which gives people the excitement. Fortunately *love* is not only for the young, it is for everyone, if only people realised that it goes on forever. Little do my children, and especially my grandchildren, know that I have been adored by men when I was young and I hope that this adulation will continue until I die. I would like to have a well attended funeral with people from all walks of life especially the medical profession who have all struggled to help me. I am very fortunate to be alive because I have had intelligent doctors who have taken an interest in my case. Of all the physical things I have lost I still have my sense of humour and the art of communication. I love people and I tell them that I love them. I have learnt this greeting from my beloved grandchildren:

'Bye, bye Gran – love you,' they tell me when I am going home. One in particular adds, 'Remember that I *still* love you.'

Since I am greatly loved by my family I want to live a little longer, and be a little stronger. Every time I 'Fall to pieces' which is one of my favourite songs I quickly remember another meaningful melody, 'Pick yourself up, dust yourself down, and start all over again'. But when I hear Frank Sinatra singing 'That's life' I get inspiration to carry on.

It is *music* which makes the world go round! Music and falling in love go hand in hand so let us all see the old year out and dance the new year in:

I hope that in 1998
Everyone will find a mate

Ode to Widows

My mother always told me when I was a child, 'Never be a widow darling, it is better to go into a convent.' I have been a widow for the past six years and believe me it does not get better, but worse! All my friends are widows and I have come to the conclusion that widows must all stick together because nobody will let us in including our own families. We always seem to be on the outside looking in!

Conversations are carried on as if we were not there and several times I have been known to return home in floods of tears from my children's houses. Exciting holiday plans are frequently discussed in front of me and if I am lucky I may get the odd invitation to tag along like a piece of baggage. It is not my children's fault because after six years they have not come to terms with the fact that I am alone and not unfortunately fancy-free. I am a widow with two children and ten grandchildren which will put any man off! However my children have a wide range of friends but neither of them have bothered to 'match make' for me and yet I am always doing this for all the lonely people I meet. I am a born matchmaker but my children have not inherited this talent which is indeed a gift. I suppose that it must be difficult for them to introduce me: 'This is my mother she suffers from loud noises in her head which drives her mad and when she gets depressed she is a crashing bore!' Who will take me on? I ask myself except a dirty old man who should be in a straitjacket. I had to break off this relationship because this man had two strong wandering hands and he was taking advantage of my loneliness. In spite of my affliction I can sing and dance and I am an excellent housekeeper. Perhaps I should advertise myself and all my widow friends in a special column in *The Times*. But I have decided to become known for my odes. Now the definition of an ode in the Oxford Dictionary is: 'Lyric poem of exalted style and tone, often of varied or irregular metre,' but my odes are my own! I have been trying to hit the jackpot for years with lengthy romantic novels, pantomimes, an unusual idea of a 'tape', love letters and an autobiography. But now I have resorted to writing short and long odes and I hope that all my widow friends will also take up a similar hobby. When our families want us to babysit we can tell them very sweetly that we cannot oblige them because we are writing our odes. If it keeps us amused I am sure our readers will laugh as well,

> Laugh and the world laughs with you
> Weep and you weep alone.

I am determined to die happy so I will continue to write my odes even if they kill me in the end. I am having five friends for coffee tomorrow morning, four of them are widows so I shall read out my 'Ode to Widows' to test their reaction.

Ode to my Birth Place

I was born in a nursing home run by nuns in Indore, a Mahratta principality of India, comprising the territories of the Holkar dynasty, and consisting of several detached tracts, covering an area of 8,402 sqm. The bulk of it lies between Sindhia's dominions on the north and Bombay Presidency on the south. It is traversed from east to west by the Nerbudda, which almost bisects it; by the Vindhya Mountains, here 2,500 feet above the sea; and by the Satpura Mountains. Principal products, poppy, cotton, tobacco, wheat, rice, millets, and; principal industries, cotton and opium manufacture. Pop. (1891) 1,094,150.

The state was founded about the middle of the eighteenth century; in 1818 its ruler became a feudatory of the British Indian empire. Indore, the capital is situated in 22 degrees 42' N. lat and 75 degrees 54' E long, 1,786 feet above sea-level. Pop. (1891) 92,329, mostly Hindus. During the revolt of 1857 though the maharaja remained faithful, his troops mutinied, holding their prince a prisoner in his own palace, and butchering many Europeans.[2]

---

[2]*Chambers Concise Gazetter of the World*, pg. 357.

I was baptised twice. My first baptism was done by a young Irish nun who gave me my first bath. I did not stop crying for hours so this nun baptised me because she thought that I might die from exhaustion. She named me Bridget Marie after her. I had an official baptism on 8 November 1923 at St Francis's Cathedral in Indore and my godparents' names were Aldolphus and Louisa Stacey, very impressive names indeed.

Ode to Order

Live in order, die in order
Live in disorder, die in chaos!

Ode to New Year's Eve

When my husband and I were young we always made a point of going out to a dinner dance on New Year's Eve. But as the years slipped by it was not possible to bring in the New Year together. He was always up in his restaurant in Hampstead but he never failed to wish me a 'Happy New Year' at midnight. I could hear the laughter and noise in the background of people bringing in the New Year but I was never jealous of his zest for the bright lights of London during the week because he always returned home on weekends.

I shall miss my husband's New Year call again this year but my thoughts are with another brave young man who will be on duty in Trafalgar Square. I do not intend to write about this young man yet, my readers will have to wait.

I have always compared myself to a lighthouse and at the moment my young policeman is picking up the threads of a shattered relationship. I shall endeavour to 'match make' for him in due course. He will have no trouble in finding a new relationship in the New Year because he is tall, dark and handsome and at only thirty years old he would be a fool to settle down. Thank God he never married his ex-girlfriend because going through a divorce would have been a harrowing experience!

Many shipwrecked young men and women have shared my lighthouse, but out of all of them I am going to miss my young policeman the most when he eventually sails away, because he came into my life when I needed him most. I was in yet another black tunnel of depression and despair. I cannot feel too blue when I hear his 'sexy' laugh which I adore!

Ode to a Flirt

Flirts play at courtship and I would like to dedicate the tune 'Flirtation' to the many flirts I have met in my life. It takes one flirt to recognise another and because flirts are attracted by flirtation they meet quite frequently. But when flirts settle down and get married they make a success of their marriages but they do not stop flirting which is absolutely harmless. I have always believed in keeping many men happy instead of making one man miserable. I married a flirt and we both allowed one another to play the field, hence no divorce. Relationships very rarely turn into passionate love affairs because flirts are not motivated by sex alone. They are normally out for a lot of fun and no harm done. There was no time for flirting when we bought a dilapidated house in Walton which had damp, dry rot and woodworm. It took us eight years of hard labour to transform it into a stately home. But it was in 'Cherwell' that I met a very sophisticated Spanish student called Cesar who was very skilful at the art of flirting.

I have dedicated an ode to him. We eventually sold 'Cherwell' and we bought a new Georgian style house in Weybridge and this was when my husband bought himself a hunting restaurant in Hampstead. We were a unique couple because we allowed one another space – he lived in Hampstead during the week and I lived in Weybridge with the children. I did all my husband's washing and ironing which he brought home on the weekends. I often think back on my social life in India but when I fell into the tender trap I ended up a flirt who irons shirts. My young policeman is also a flirt but he irons his own shirts. There is no fear of an Oedipus relationship because at seventy-four he will not knock on my bedroom door. Of that I am sure!

Ode to my Father

My beloved father was born on 23 April 1882 in a place called Amraoti in India. Rumour had it that his father Marc came from a titled family. But the family got into debt and consequently they could not keep up their vast estate or pay their taxes. Marc and his brother decided to leave Portugal, they boarded a ship in Rotterdam and changed the family name to Alberts and sailed to India. The brothers jumped ship at Goa, one brother became a priest and Marc met and married a beautiful Spanish girl called Sophia Madeira. They had two children, Claude, my father, and Mary his sister. Marc worked as a clerk in what I presume was the Portuguese Embassy. The children were very well educated and talented. My father who was born on Shakespeare's birthday was a man of words and music and he composed a song for every child except me because he knew that I was the dancer of the family, and I believe I used to dance for him from eleven months old. I was always crying and in order to soothe my tears he would tell my mother, 'Take her clothes off, she is too hot,' and then he would play his guitar and I would dance.

My father was a Conservator of Forests for The Maharaja of Holkar, a very wealthy Indian state and I was his youngest harem dancer! His sister Mary moved to Calcutta when she got married.

It was in Calcutta that my father met my English mother. He was visiting his sister Mary at the time when he found his bride to be at Mass on a Sunday. I believe that he could not take his eyes off my mother because she was so beautiful. Her glorious auburn hair which was her crowning glory caught his eye as the sun beamed through the stained glass windows of the church and he peeped at her through his open fingers, head bowed down as he pretended to pray. After the service was over he took note of her name from the family pew and he asked the Parish priest to introduce him to Annie Lydia Lewis. My mother who had twice been engaged to Englishmen always broke off her engagements at the last minute because she was not prepared to leave her mother. It was my father's passionate love letters which finally made up her mind to leave home. My parents married in Calcutta on 25 May 1916 at the church of the Sacred Heart, 3 Dharrumtola Street, Calcutta. My father took his beautiful bride back to Mhow where he had a house. My father was thirty-four years old and my mother was twenty-five when they got married, but this blissfully happy marriage ended in tragedy when my father died of a stroke at the age of forty-two, leaving my heart-broken mother a widow at the age of thirty-four with five daughters to struggle on alone. My brother was born six months after my father's death. There would be no more glamorous garden parties or balls at the palace for Annie or a house full of servants at her beck and call. It was going to be tough because widowhood in India is vastly different from England with all the social services! There would be no more exciting tiger shoots or watching her husband play a game of polo with the Prince of Wales when he came out to India.

My mother fell in love with the young Prince of Wales when she met him at a garden party and she never forgave him for marrying Mrs Simpson, her father was English so she was a staunch royalist. My father had trained my mother to use a rifle skilfully and when she was blamed for sending a servant to his death in order to retrieve a duck she had shot down, my father fought her case for her and won. It must have been tragic to see a faithful servant gradually being swallowed up in sinking sand. My mother was pointing her gun at him asking him to grab hold of it so that she could pull him out but the evil press turned the tables on her. I believe his last words were: 'Salaam Memsahib,' and he gave her a loyal salute and disappeared. She loved this servant who had been on many shoots with my parents.

My brave father had to travel on an elephant and sometimes

by bullock-cart in the dense forests. He often had to leave my mother behind with the servants but he always tried to return on a Sunday to play the organ in church. He told the Parish priest that one day he would have all his daughters singing in the church choir. Little did he know it then that his five daughters did become famous singers during the war but they gave their services free for sweet, sweet, charity! Mhow was a first class military station so the British soldiers often harassed my beautiful mother when my father was on tour.

'Shoot the blighters near their feet,' he told her which she did and it soon made the cowards run away.

My father had several soldiers in the church choir and they came to our house for choir practice. An amusing incident took place one day when a soldier arrived with a thick love letter. My father asked who it was for and the poor love sick man pointed to my mother who had just walked into the room. I would have loved to have seen my father's face when he handed the letter to my mother, I believe she accepted it with a smile! She was accustomed to the soldiers getting a crush on her.

I feel very close to my father's spirit today. It has been a horrible day, we have had heavy rain and 'Stormy weather' like the song. I feel very alone because my young policeman has gone out to his club and my daughter has gone down to her home in Alderburgh. But my grandson, James, may come to see me later. He has been popping in to see me the last two days as he is very interested in my odes. He knows my romantic character well and we both share a few secrets. It seems just the other day he was a baby, how the years have flown because he is nineteen years old now.

I shall conclude my ode to my father saying that I still desperately need a man like him. A strong, yet romantic man, because I also need to be wooed with 'Love letters straight from the heart' which is yet another song!

Ode to my Sisters and Brother

I am going to compare my sisters and brother to precious jewels.

Pearl, my eldest sister Mary, was very frail. Her transparent skin was like a pearl. She had brown eyes, a few freckles on her delicate face and gorgeous auburn hair. She should have married an army officer and remained in India. She is a widow now and she lives in Devon.

Ruby, my second eldest sister, Norine, was exotic. She had perfect Latin features, brown eyes and a lovely olive complexion. She was the lead singer. Ruby should have continued her singing career. If she had married a man who was a good manager she could still be singing today. Ruby is a widow as well and she lives in Sydney, Australia.

Opal, my third eldest sister, Olive, like my brother is a good musician. She still plays the piano or organ for the church functions. Opal, like the jewel was very pretty. She had a fair skin freckled face and beautiful auburn hair. She is also a widow and she lives in Sydney, Australia.

Emerald, my fourth eldest sister, Lynette, was very witty and attractive. She, like the other two auburn-haired sisters had a scattering of freckles. Emerald's dark brown eyes are her best feature because they are heavily lashed. Emerald is still a State Registered Nurse in America. She does private work now and she lives in California and whenever I hear 'California Blues' my thoughts rush back to Emerald. She is a widow as well.

I am the diamond, the priceless Koh-in-Noor! I am the fifth girl, the enigma or 'spice girl' of the family. When I was born my father's salary doubled so he called me the lucky baby. I am very lucky to be alive because I have always had bad health due to emotional problems. When I was young I had luxurious raven hair, sparkling hazel eyes, a few freckles and a lightly tanned complexion. During the war all the boys told me that I looked like Hedy Lamarr, a film actress.

Copper, my brother, Claude is still very handsome. He looks a lot like my father. I have named him Copper because when he got his demob from the RAF in London he emigrated to Rhodesia and he got a job in the Copper mines. Copper, like myself, has my father's Latin temperament, we both like moonlight, music and romance, the song is 'Let's face the music and dance'!

It is still raining 'Pennies from heaven' which I hope is a good omen! Since this is my story I shall only briefly mention my family.

Ode to my Mother

How can I describe my mother? The nuns in school and everyone who met her told us, 'Your mother is a lady to her fingertips.'

She was a lady, very feminine, and she wore hats and silk stockings even on the hottest day. She was a very fashionable woman and her vast trousseau consisted of forty-two pairs of shoes and hats. She was a typical English Memsahib and sometimes I saw a poor beggar kiss her feet when she gave him or her some money which embarrassed her very much. People loved her and when we children went out shopping with her, often all dressed alike, we used to be counted by the shop keepers who spoilt us with sweets. India is a land of children and my brother was undoubtedly everyone's favourite and we all loved him very much because he was a boy. Our house was always full of music and dancing. My mother's favourite tune was 'The Blue Danube' and she taught us all how to do the waltz.

'Bend backwards, do not lean forwards,' she told us and once she whispered, 'You know darling I would get up from my grave if I heard "The Blue Danube" and waltz into heaven'.

Ironically I often think that I may have to cha, cha, cha! to hell in the near future but not yet because I have not quite finished my job here on earth. My mother and her three sisters went to grand balls when they were young ladies and they were known as the four graces!

My mother told me that the men had to book a dance in advance and they often dangled their invitation cards on their wrists. How enchanting! I remember my mother taking my eldest sister to her first ball. She always wore simple black dresses to balls when she became a widow but my sister wore a gorgeous red taffeta dress and I did her hair in ringlets for her. She looked exquisite. It was an officers' ball but my sister secretly invited her dancing partner who was a sergeant and he had the nerve to borrow an officer's jacket and turn up. He did not fool my mother who asked him sternly, 'Since when have you become an officer, Maxwell? I shall report you to your Commanding Officer if you don't leave now.'

Poor Maxwell was too ashamed to reply but my sister spoke up for him, 'Please, Mummy, please let me dance the Charleston with Maxwell and then he will leave.'

Maxwell and my eldest sister were superb Charleston dancers. She met Maxwell at one of the church hops. All of us learnt how to dance from the British Tommies at these hops but only army officers were good enough as prospective husbands in my mother's eyes. She had an eye on a handsome young Sandhurst officer for her eldest daughter. Sadly poor Maxwell left the ball after the Charleston was over on his bicycle and my mother and my eldest sister proudly drove home in Ronald Patterson's smart Ford! If only my eldest sister had listened to my mother she could have had a wonderful life in India as an army officer's wife because Ronald remained out in India for many years. We saw his wedding picture many years later in the *Tatler* and he returned to India with his English bride where they may still be living.

I remember the sleepless nights my mother had thinking about her future.

'Why are you not sleeping, Mummy?' I asked her several times.

'I am thinking about my bills,' she would reply. 'I must be very careful of your father's hard-earned money, it must last me a lifetime,' and it did because when my beloved mother died we all got equal shares. I was very close to my mother and she often told me that I had my father's hazel eyes and his beautiful feet. Unfortunately my mother had ruined her feet by squeezing her toes into fashionable pointed shoes. I have also done many foolish things which I now regret. There is a saying, 'Woman thy name is vanity', and that is *me*!

I wish I could have another tummy tuck because a plastic surgeon has ruined me. I never knew that he was a boob and nose man, I should have had him struck off for the mess he made. Why am I still so vain?

Ode to a Policeman

My handsome young policeman flew off to Canada this morning for a skiing holiday in Vancouver. I left him a note in the kitchen, 'Have a happy holiday. Take care of yourself.' and his reply was charming,

'Thank you! I'll have a great time, but I won't have my landlady to look after me.'

It must be very exciting to be thirty years old and to be tall, dark and handsome flying off in a party of seven to Canada, by comparison I at seventy-four am doing my weekly wash including my policeman's bed linen. I have the radio on and when I heard Roy Orbison's lovely song 'In dreams' I had to get up and dance because the rhythm was fantastic. I began to dream about my young policeman in Canada wishing that I was twenty-four on a skiing holiday with him.

I am feeling very romantic this morning, the sun is shining and it could easily be spring! My young policeman does not know how to dance and on his return from Canada it will be a great pleasure to teach him. It is a great drawback if a man cannot dance because most love affairs begin with music and dancing. I am going to give a farewell party for him and I have got my eye on a couple of foreign girls I want to introduce him to before he moves on to the new house he has bought himself.

God sent this young policeman into my life when I needed him most, he is responsible for my odes because when I am happy I write to music. I may be in love again! I fell madly in love with the moon last night and this morning I am in love with the sun. I am in love with life!

I do not know how to ski but I am sure that if I was twenty-four I would soon learn if I had a handsome policeman to pick me up every time I fell. I wonder who the lucky girl is going to be who is going to fall into his arms on this winter holiday? I wish him love, he deserves a new romance! People do not realise how lucky we are in England to have such a marvellous Police Force, they are so brave. Soldiers only fight when we have a war but our policemen have to deal with domestic quarrels everyday.

Yesterday I noticed that his lovely brown eyes were 'misty' like the song, he looked so romantic but when I heard that CS gas was responsible for his blurred vision I was very concerned.

Criminals are so violent nowadays so our policemen have to use equally violent deterrents sometimes harming themselves as well. This young man has definitely been my best lodger and I have been taking in lodgers for many years. He is polite, very reserved and he keeps his work apart from his private life so I do not know much about his job. But I do see how tired he looks sometimes when he returns home, he usually goes straight to his room to relax. A talkative landlady is the last thing he wants after the traumas of the day so I began writing my odes.

I shall give this ode to my policeman as a parting present with a hand carved lighthouse in wood which is painted red and white with a vivid blue sky in the background. He can hang it up in his new house. I hope that it will be a lasting souvenir of his stay with me. The Ode to Cesar was about an Oedipus love affair which happens once in a life time. I may tell my readers about it sometime! I know that I am in love again but with who, *That is the question?*

Ode to Birdie House

I hate winter so I am going to go back in time to my roots in India where I was born and brought up. When my father died we became poor and my beloved widowed mother rented a little bungalow. It was called 'Birdie House'. It was a very humble dwelling but it was full of joy and happiness during our school holidays. It was occupied by a sad swallow who was my mother and six chicks: five female and one male. It had one small veranda, one dining room and one large room which was divided into half by a partition in order to make a drawing room and a bedroom.

The bedroom had seven camp cots or stretchers which we all slept on, the light mattresses were cosy and the beds were spotlessly clean with just a couple of sheets and a pillow. The bathroom was also divided into a bathing area and a loo.

The loo had seven wooden thrones, a large one for my mother and the other ones varied in size according to our age. My wooden throne was next to Lynette's and I must recall a very amusing incident which I still remember. One day when we were both sitting comfortably Lynette decided to put her lid down because she was about to leave the loo when I heard her shriek.

'I saw something move!' she exclaimed in horror, and I being very inquisitive jumped up from my throne to see what it was. To my horror I realised that it was my poor mynah bird covered in pooh! I quickly recovered the old bird and rushed over to the bathing area to wash it. I have always had high standards of hygiene and I wanted my bird to be scrupulously clean and I think I over bathed it. I dried it lovingly with an old towel and I put it back in its cage. That summer holiday Olive, Lynette and I bought ourselves mynahs and I was given the oldest bird because I was the youngest. My poor mother had to put up with three talkative daughters trying to teach three mynah birds to talk!

Sadly I found my mynah bird lying stiff in its cage the following morning. It had obviously died of pneumonia. The funeral was very sad because I could not stop crying. My brother Claude was the priest and I being the chief mourner was supported by Lynette who had caused the death of my mynah and Olive also attended the funeral. My two eldest sisters never played with us. They were too interested in boyfriends! We buried my poor mynah in the compound and Claude marked the grave with a little wooden cross. I will always associate 'Birdie House' with the short life and death of my mynah bird.

During the hot weather we all slept out in the compound on our stretchers in the bright moonlight. Perhaps this could be the reason why I am an incurable romantic. One lovely tropical moonlit night a drunk British solider sat on Olive's stretcher and began running his hands up and down her thighs and she was still fast asleep but the dogs raised the alarm and our next door neighbour who had been a British solider soon saw him off. This poor man was blind but he had a voice as loud as thunder. When he left the army he became a ticket collector on the railways. Rumour had it that he turned a beggar out of the train because he did not have a ticket and the man put a curse on him and he became totally blind.

Sleeping out in summer under a canopy of stars and a tropical moon is out of this world but when it rained it was a different story because we had to carry our stretchers which was hard work. As usual Olive invariably slept through the rain and we had to shake her to wake her up. We had a much loved dog, his name was Mickey and a mongrel stray called Teddy, they used to dig themselves into little holes for the night as they kept guard on us. I would like to see 'Birdie House' again one day, it was almost opposite the convent I used to attend. It must be sad and lonely without us!

Ode to St Joseph's Convent

My first boarding school convent was in Jubbulpore, it was called St Joseph's Convent. My mother had decided to move her daughters to the hills because my two eldest sisters were getting very fond of the college boys, thereby neglecting their studies. My eldest sister's school report was the final straw that broke the camel's back. It read: 'Mary is more interested in reading romantic novels than doing her homework'.

I have only seen my beloved mother once in a temper in my life and it was when she got this bad report about her eldest daughter. She took a stick and whacked my sister on her legs.

'Education is the finest thing a parent can give a child' she told Mary firmly.

'Your father made me promise to educate all of you. My sisters and I were turned away from school because my English father was a drunkard and he couldn't pay the school fees,' she told us.

Mary never shed a tear and she almost defied my ladylike mother to beat her again but I broke down, 'Mummy darling please stop beating Mary please stop for my sake,' I cried.

When she saw how distressed I was she sat down quietly and I ran into her arms. This dramatic outburst was the beginning of a new life for us girls. St Joseph's Convent in the plains could not compete with the convents in the hills. The food was awful. We ate boiled onions on Fridays for dinner. The Catholic Church brought this dogma in to conserve stocks of meat for the clergy! The girls were multi-racial. There were no private bathrooms only one huge public room where we girls had to bathe with wrappers on, supervised by a nun. It was very funny to see the girls with big boobs jump about under the fierce taps, their bosoms would wobble like jellies! I found a nice secluded tap and I made sure I soaped myself under and over my bathing wrapper so that I would be clean all over.

Head lice became an epidemic and I was best lice catcher in the school so I had many clients, especially the girls who had very long hair. I skilfully pulled the knits out squashing them with my thumb nails. There was great activity every morning because we had to turn our mattresses every day and heaven help the girl who wet her bed. One poor girl wet her bed every night and she was made to stand in the study hall every morning with her sheet on her head. I still remember her night prayer, 'Please Jesus don't let me wet my bed tonight.' She repeated this simple request fervently several times but Jesus never heard her prayer but I did and now I am going to expose cruel Catholic nuns because Jesus has told me to do so. I do not hear voices like Joan of Arc but my conscience tells me to write the truth. I wet my bed once when I was in the infirmary but I did it deliberately. I was sick with a nervous skin rash at the same time as a dirty little boy called Malcolm. I wanted to go to the loo one day and when I approached the door it was open and there was this scruffy little devil sitting on the loo rolling up his shoe laces.

'What are you going to do with that?' I asked pointing to the worm-like thing in his hand.

'I am going to wipe my bottom,' he replied cheekily and I fled in horror!

The next day he craftily locked the loo door refusing to let me in so I went back to my room and spent an unending penny in my bed because I did not want to make a puddle on the floor. I was very ashamed of myself and I cried bitterly, the nun in the infirmary dried my tears. She tried to comfort me.

'It wasn't your fault. It was Malcolm's fault, he played a dirty trick on you,' she told me kindly. I hated this little boy because I was in love with Monsignor Doubleman and the school doctor.

'Take off all her clothes,' the school doctor said to the narrow-minded nun in the infirmary. 'How can I examine her rash?' he asked impatiently. He had had one too many at lunch I could smell gin on his breath as he examined me. I lay on the bed stark naked and the handsome doctor with his twinkling gin and tonic eyes ran his hands up and down my frail body. I began to giggle because I was watching the nun's horrified face.

'Send her home to her mother where she belongs,' he told the nun. I loved this doctor because he sent me home once before when my brother was ill with pneumonia because his illness upset me. He also told Mother Superior off in front of me after a school concert.

'You are expecting too much from this child, she is suffering from nervous exhaustion. Send her home.'

My beloved mother always turned up like a fairy godmother with her familiar handbag to take me home, leaving my sisters behind to finish the term. She once bought me a whole new wardrobe of matching dresses like hers: rich Aunt Violet lured me into a boarding school. I was playing in the compound when I overheard an intimate conversation.

'Why is Bridget not in boarding school?' she asked my mother anxiously and I heard my mother reply,

'The doctor has told me not to send Bridget away as a boarder because she will die.'

'Nonsense,' said Aunt Violet. 'I'll soon tempt her with pretty dresses to go to school.'

Aunt Violet was right. My pretty dresses made me feel beautiful and this is why I fell in love twice!

When I first met Sister Ernestine, a French nun in St Joseph's Convent in Jubbulpore I was terrified of her because she was an ogre. She was an old nun so her teaching days were over but her shadow walking down the long corridors could frighten a little girl to death. I clearly remember her pulling out a young teenager making a spectacle of her in the study hall which was Sister Ernestine's domain because she had worn a little make-up one day. This girl was a day scholar but she vented her anger on her. She made her kneel down in the middle of the hall so that we were all able to see her and then she slapped her face from side to side.

'You are a bold brazen hussy,' she said out aloud. 'Now wash your face.' She handed her a bowl of water and a towel and forced this girl to carry out her command. This vivacious girl had taught us how to do 'the carioca' during our break which was a Brazilian dance and she had painted her face that day but she forgot to remove her lipstick. It was almost the end of term and we were all in high spirits because Carmen Miranda's dancing had impressed many girls and I was one of them. Tragically after this innocent incident this young girl who was a superb dancer was killed on her boyfriend's motorbike before we broke up. I like to think that Sister Ernestine did not break her zest for fun and we all mourned her death because she was a popular character.

However Sister Ernestine and I became good friends in the end because at the age of eight I carried a big wooden chair for her and I came tumbling down the concrete steps cutting my chin very badly. I almost bled to death because the cut was very deep but I never shed a tear. I was too scared to cry because I thought that Sister Ernestine would slap my face as well! After my brave deed she allowed me to hold on to her tassel when we walked down the dingy corridors. I think she was afraid of the dark and so was I. When it rained and thundered as it did frequently during the monsoons she said out aloud in the silent study hall, 'And the word was made flesh,' and we all had to reply in unison, 'And dwelt amongst us.'

Quite amusing when I think back on it now but very eerie at the time. The lightening and storms were fearful in Jubbulpore during the monsoon.

Father Roen was a tyrant! He was a Dutchman and he was the headmaster of the boys' college next door to St Joseph's Convent. This priest was evil, far worse than Sister Ernestine, and all the boys hated his guts. He was a woman hater! He grabbed hold of me one evening when I was distributing the rosaries at Benediction. He pulled me out of the aisle and made me kneel down in front of Our Lady's statue with my arms outstretched during the whole of the service which was a very long time for a little girl. The tears rolled down my face like rivers and the pain in my frail arms was excruciating. I am sure that Father Roen thought that I was distributing love letters from the boys to the senior girls. As soon as a girl began menstruating black socks were changed to black stockings so the boys got the signal and the church became a kind of dating place and we little girls got caught up when 'love was in the air'!

I often kept 'KV' when my two eldest sisters were talking to their college boyfriends.

Father Roen made a fool of himself on one feast day when he came across to the convent dressed up as a nun. When I come to think of it who dressed this demon up? A nun's habit is very difficult to put on, perhaps he was having fun and games with Sister Ernestine? He could not fool me because his black beard kept popping out. It was a brave mother who eventually gave this Dutch bully his just dues. He had flogged her son for some petty offence so she marched up to his office and picked up his pet cat and threw it out of the window and it died instantly. I felt sorry for the cat but it was a great tribute to a mother's courage! Father Roen was a toad.

I was seven years old when I was chosen to greet Monsignor Doubleman at Jubbulpore station on his return from Rome where the Pope had made him a Monsignor. I remember standing with a nun shaking with fright with a bouquet of flowers which was almost as big as myself! As the train came gently to a halt I walked towards Monsignor Doubleman's carriage. I gave a little curtsey as I approached him and I kissed his ring which had a large purple stone. I shall never forget this distinguished priest's radiant smile as I did this gesture and when I saw his face light up I fell madly in love with him. There is a song called 'Now it can be told' which is not a favourite of mine but very apt because it describes my emotions perfectly. My father might have been my first love but Monsignor Doubleman was undoubtedly the kind of man I would adore. He was very handsome and I likened him to Jesus Christ and I was a very young Mary Magdalen. Falling in love is so precious and it can and does happen to anyone regardless of age.

Monsignor Doubleman and I met again a short time later during a procession when I was a flower girl.

I did a ballet of my own specially for him as I threw rose petals in his path when he was carrying the Blessed Sacrament and he in return gave me 'that certain smile' which told me that I had done my job well. A man's smile can say so much to a woman especially an emotional person like me and when I am not depressed I smile at everyone. I love the song called 'Smile' it has beautiful meaningful words. I often smile at myself in the mirror with the tears rolling down my cheeks. I say 'Goodnight' to myself when I am alone but now I have lodgers I say 'Good morning' and 'Goodnight' to them!

As I write my story my readers will soon realise that all human beings need to be loved otherwise they will wither and die. No man is an Island and I hope that I am going to find someone like Monsignor Doubleman one day because he was so kind to me. I cannot live alone, I need people, not just a pen and paper for my companions, as I journey towards the end of my life. I miss my husband terribly and my children are too busy leading their own lives. Perhaps I should become a housekeeper to a cardinal or a monsignor because a spiritual relationship can go on forever?

Ode to Menstruation

I had been looking after three little orphan children during the summer holidays. As soon as I heard that their mother had died I scaled the wall between 'Birdie House' and their home. I jumped into their garden like a peasblossom fairy to take care of the children. Their grandmother and maiden aunt were having difficulty in keeping them amused because they were missing their mother very much. I put the three of them in their large pram and I wheeled the heavy pram into our compound. They shrieked with delight when I wheeled them up and down a little slope and because it made them happy I struggled along doing this for quite a long time.

Olive and Lynette were playing with their dolls, Olive was Mrs Norma Shearer. Lynette was Mrs Betty Davis and they wanted me to be Mrs Gloria Swanson. Poor Claude was also dragged into the game and he was Lynette's dog, she walked him on his hands and knees and she even put a lead round his neck which I thought was very cruel. Since I would not join in the game preferring to do something useful Olive, Lynette and Claude mocked me chanting in unison, 'Here comes Granny' laughing their heads off as I fought back my tears but I never let them get the better of me. When I was a child I was very sensitive and any member of my family could make me cry instantly by pointing a finger at me and saying, 'Poor Beedie Bumty!'

The tears flowed like rivers. Claude was the main culprit because he loved teasing me but it never stopped me from loving him because he was a boy! Claude's teasing was playful but Mary could be cruel; she gave me the ruler in school if she thought I had been rude to one of her friends. She once threw a shoe at me when I was packing my trunk for Nazareth Convent Ootacmund. The buckle cut open a very sensitive area just under my nose and I still have the scar. I almost bled to death and my mother had to rush to help me with a damp handkerchief which she held on the deep wound until it stopped bleeding. She gave Mary a good telling off and then she asked me, 'Does Mary hit you in school?'

'Yes,' I replied. 'I dare not be cheeky to any of her friends because she takes me to the loo and she whacks me with a ruler.'

'You will not hit Bridget in the new school Mary,' said my mother sternly. 'I shall be very cross with you if you do,' she added.

I was dreading going to Nazareth Convent because it meant leaving my beloved mother for nine months. Besides I was afraid of being cold in the hills.

'Mummy, darling,' I told my mother every day please don't send me to the hills I will die of the cold.'

I cried for a week repeating this same request.

'Let my sisters go but not me, please Mummy, please!' but her reply was cool.

'You can cry for a week darling,' which is exactly what I did 'But you are going to Nazareth Convent with your sisters.'

I am afraid that looking after three orphan children, the sadness of leaving our sweeper woman's baby and finally jumping on a huge bandicoot in the dining room was responsible for making mother nature wake up during that long hot summer. We were all sitting in the dining room having our dinner when a huge bandicoot appeared running across the room. Everyone shrieked and stood on their chairs and my mother calmly got up and instructed Claude to kill it. Claude was chasing it all around the room missing it by inches so I decided to jump on it and I stood there terrified until its last squeak. All the family gave me a standing ovation.

'Three cheers for Beedie Bumty,' they said in unison.

'Hip, hip, hooray!'

When all the confusion was over I suddenly got a bad tummy ache and I went to the loo to spend a penny. When I saw the loo paper I got the fright of my life.

'Mummy, Mummy,' I screamed. 'I am bleeding to death. You cannot send me to Nazareth Convent,' I cried hysterically.

My mother came into the loo and tried to calm me down.

'You are not bleeding to death,' she reassured me. 'You have begun menstruating.'

'What's that?' I asked innocently.

'You have got your periods,' she replied.

'And what is a period?' I asked in between sobs.

'It is something all grown-up girls get every month!' she said.

'No, Mummy I do not want to get my periods because I don't want to be grown up,' I cried.

'Calm down, darling. I'll fetch Norine and she will tell you all about it because she's got her periods at the moment.'

As soon as Norine came into the loo I gave her a hug. 'Please Norine, Mummy says that you are menstruating. Can I have a look?'

Norine smiled sweetly and pulled up her dress and showed me her knickers and I could see that she had a sanitary towel on. My mother left the loo and Norine folded a snow-white sanitary towel and pinned it to the elastic belt she had put round my waist.

'I hate it Norine. I hate being harnessed like an animal. Look it is poking out from my dress and I cannot walk,' I shouted impatiently.

'Take it off,' said Norine patiently. 'I'll make it smaller,' and she folded the muslin towel yet again.

'Why do we have to get periods, Norine?' I asked her.

'Well the only alternative is to have a baby,' she said laughing at me.

'I am going to have many babies,' I replied 'like our methrani,' (sweeper woman) and I continued, 'I have used these muslin cloths many times on her baby.'

'Don't worry she won't mind,' said Ruby, 'because the methrani washes our sanitary towels before they go to the dhobi (man who washes clothes).'

Ode to a Methrani

Our poor methrani has an awful life because she also empties our potties and washes them twice a day, I thought.

But when I came to England I soon realised that I was a 'Jill of all trades'. In other words I was a cook, a bearer (butler) a washer-up, an ayah (nanny), a dhobi (man who washes clothes) and a methrani (a woman who cleans the toilet and sweeps).

Our methrani was exquisitely beautiful. She wore very colourful saris and cholis (blouses) and her graceful movements when she was sweeping the compound drew my attention to her and I often did a little sweeping for her. She wore pretty glass bangles, hooped gold earrings and a gold stud in her nose. Her complexion was a golden brown unlike that of the metha (sweeper) who was black. Norine told me that our sweeper woman was not married to the metha but that they were living together.

How modern, I thought to myself, but when I was young and foolish I definitely wanted to get married. This beautiful woman must have had a very interesting life! She was not an untouchable or a low caste but she obviously fell in love with the sweeper and she set up home with him which was a mud hut in our compound. I was a frequent visitor to her hut because I loved her children, and she never failed to give me a new baby every year. I loved our methrani's babies because they were very bonny. They normally wore no clothes just a black string round their fat tummies and their huge eyes were outlined with kohl. I often brought back a baby to 'Birdie House' bathed and powered the child then I took the little one back to the methrani's hut in a snow white nappy which I later discovered were muslin sanitary towels. I saw my sweeper woman's children twice a year when we went to St Joseph's Convent in Jubbulpore but when I was sent to the hills I only saw them once a year. I remember saying a sad farewell to our beautiful methrani and I whispered:

'Don't forget to have a new baby for me on my return from school,' and she shook her head and twinkled her eyes which meant – Yes!

Ode to Nazareth Convent, Ootacmund

The train journey from Mhow in Central India to Ootacmund in the south of India was a very long tedious one. It took approximately two nights and three days. The journey to St Joseph's Convent in Jubbulpore by comparison was short, and being in the plains the scenery was not very spectacular except for the dramatic sight of the Western Ghats which were huge waterfalls.

My mother saw us off at the station and we all crowded around her to kiss her goodbye. As usual I was in floods of tears. Mary however was having a very exciting time because Ronald Patterson had decided to race his Ford for as long as possible alongside the train. I was waving goodbye to my mother until I gradually saw her solitary figure disappear in a sea of black faces then I went across to Mary's side of the train and I caught a glimpse of handsome Ronald waving his Panama hat when he was forced to stop at a level crossing. I felt sad to see these young lovers parting as I often swept the court in the compound for them to play badminton.

Indian trains are like huge monsters and our family has travelled hundreds of miles on them to the north, south, east and west of India either going to school or visiting relatives and friends. When we all grew up and got jobs we went on our annual holidays by train to the seaside or the hills. When I think back on this long journey to Ootacmund we were very brave girls to have undertaken this journey alone. We did not travel in the comfort of a first or second class compartment like the school batch because we were in an overcrowded third class carriage with female natives. One year on our return journey home when there was no room for us with the women we travelled in the men's compartment. These men were delighted to have us.

We even changed into our pyjamas at night like nicely brought up convent girls. When I was a child I liked travelling in a third class carriage because train journeys can get very boring but when we grew up we did travel second class on our joint holidays. Looking back on our lives we were a united bunch of sisters. Lynette was a nurse and it was sometimes difficult for her to join the four of us who were all secretaries.

Indians are great travellers and they always seem to be going back and forth to their villages taking all their worldly goods with them. Since I love people I soon made friends with mothers and babies in order to try and forget my own mother. Going to Nazareth Convent meant that we would be in boarding school for nine months and we would return home for three months each year. It was very cruel to send a child away for such a long period, especially to a convent, where we were at the mercy of Catholic nuns. As the train travelled south I noticed that the natives became darker and when we reached Madras the people were very black and the language had changed from Hindi to Tamil which was very difficult to understand. Meals on Indian trains can be ordered from the dining car, little bearers rushed about delivering the food on trays but if one wished one could go to the dining car when the train stopped at a station and have it in style. None of this appealed to me as a child because I preferred my mother's delicious hamper in a picnic basket on our journey to school and Nazareth Convent's equally good food on our journey home.

We eventually changed trains to a narrow gauge train in order to climb the Nilgri Hills. The toy trains to the hills with the spectacular scenery was like being lifted from earth to paradise! As the train meandered up the hills the eucalyptus trees with their lovely silver trunks stood silently like smartly dressed convent girls, cool and orderly on the outside but smouldering volcanoes on the inside. Convent girls are allowed to smoulder but we were *never* allowed to erupt!

India owes Britain a great debt for the railways especially the narrow gauge trains which are an amazing feat of British engineering. The hairpin bends are hair raising and when the climb becomes too steep a cog line appears in the centre and one can feel the shunting movement which made me feel sick, and the cold and the altitude made me feel faint. In some hill stations the train is pulled by one steam engine in the front and pushed from the back by another. These unique little toy trains did a grand job getting everyone safely to their destinations in the hills.

We were met at Ootacmund station by a nun and we were driven away in the school car to Nazareth Convent where I spent three of the most formative years of my life! A young girl soon learns about life between the ages of thirteen and fifteen especially about how the other half of the world lives! As soon as we arrived at Nazareth Convent we met Mother Chad, the English headmistress, in the parlour. All convents have grand parlours including St Joseph's Convent in Jubbulpore. The parlours were very tastefully furnished but none of them could be compared to Nazareth Convent's. On our arrival we were given a delicious hot meal and then the nannies took us to the bathrooms for a lovely hot bath but again we were handed the usual wrapper in spite of the fact that we had private bathrooms which had modern enamel bath tubs. The notorious bathing wrapper was responsible for turning me into a glorified nun! But I have been told by a wise monsignor in Weybridge that nuns know all about masturbation, they confess this sin regularly yet they never wanted us to discover our own sexuality. Normal people want to fall in love like the song 'Let's do it let's fall in love' but nuns are not normal.

After our baths we were taken to our cubicles in the dormitory. Public dormitories were replaced by private cubicles, these cubicles had no doors just curtains which were drawn back at night and opened in the morning.

I was very lucky because my cubicle was opposite Sister Bianca's room, she was the little Italian nun in charge of the dormitory. I adored this charming nun who was very fond of me because she understood my Latin character. I loved wishing her on her feast day.

'Happy feast Sister Bianca,' I told her.

'And the same to you,' was her delightful reply.

The Catholic Church has not canonised me yet but I hope my book which is a true story will make the church change some of their man-made rules. We did not have plumbed-in basins in our cubicles like the parlour boarders, we only had China jugs filled with water which stood in a China bowl. We used to wash our faces first in ice cold water and then we cleaned our teeth. We filled our tooth mugs with water after brushing our teeth with toothpaste and spat into the bowl before going to Mass every morning. We had luxurious hot baths about three times a week which I loved because they helped to warm up my ice cold body. Our clean clothes were neatly wrapped in a bath towel by the nannies.

Nazareth Convent had all it's priorities right. Most of the girls were English, we also had a few diplomats' daughters from the Foreign Embassies. We did have one Indian girl, her father was a very important man in The Bank of India. Tragically this very talented girl took her own life many years later and her body was found floating down the Saint Lawrence river in America. I met her mother once in the New Market in Calcutta but I did not have the courage to find out why her only daughter had committed suicide. She played the violin beautifully. We also had a young Indian prince and a princess. They were the Maharaja of Mysore's children, we called them Jack and Jill.

We visited their father's winter palace in Ooty once and as I ran through the long corridors near the women's quarters I thought of my father because I believe the harem girls always recognised his footsteps in the palace when he was a Forest Officer for the Maharaja of Holkar.

Rich Parsee girls – girls of Persian extraction – were also

boarders, they had their own dining room and dormitories. Parlour boarders had lovely rooms with private nannies. I became friends with a parlour boarder and she asked Sister Bianca if I could spend the last night in her room one year before we broke up. I thoroughly enjoyed the luxury. It was in Nazareth Convent that I came to realise that I had a popular personality but Mother Chad was determined to cut me down to size. She chiselled at what was once a sparkling Koh-in-Noor diamond and turned me into a 'solitaire' like the song! But not for long because it was in this posh school full of rich children I developed into a unique individual, meaning I could mix with the rich and since there were no poor children I learnt how to act like the rich! I now have two rich children who are a credit to me and one day I know I shall be rich like my children from sheer hard work.

I had no pretty dresses in Nazareth Convent which drew Monsignor Doubleman's attention to me and I was not allowed to flirt with the school doctor either because Mother Chad kept him for herself. I often saw her swanning around the school corridors with him but she would not let him examine me when I complained about terrible tummy aches during my periods. I remember being put to bed one day in the infirmary with a hot water bottle because I was in agony and Mother Chad paid me a surprise visit.

'I'm sorry for giving you a telling off this morning at assembly. I thought you looked far too young to be having period pains,' she said quite kindly.

I was fourteen years old at the time but it was true that I did look very young because my boobs were tiny rosebuds. But I did play netball in the senior team from the age of thirteen because I was an excellent 'shoot'. Mother Chad was very proud of me during the school matches because Nazareth Convent won all the matches in the Nilgri Hills and she actually paid me a compliment.

'You should think seriously of taking up netball professionally,' she told me one day after a match. 'I am very proud of you.'

I have my father's hazel eyes and he was the best marksman in his regiment in the war in Mesopotamia so scoring goals was very easy for me. I loved scoring the penalty 'free shots' because I always got the ball straight into the net and I got a loud applause. Olive played centre and Lynette played defence and we three sisters were a great credit to Nazareth Convent. Our competitors always turned up in snazzy shorts but it was the convent girls with their long gymslips who won all the games and prizes. I got a crush on my history teacher in Nazareth Convent, she was also our games mistress because she wore lovely clothes and I thought to myself, One day when I grow up I am going to have beautiful clothes like Miss Taylor, and I did!

However in Nazareth Convent I was given a worn out two-toned gym slip. It was light brown in the front and dark brown at the back so in order not to draw attention to this tatty gymslip I walked about the school with my arms straight down my sides. Nuns can be very cruel! I blamed Mother Chad for my humiliation because she was the headmistress. The uniforms were imported from England and so were most of the girls but we five sisters gave this school some spice!

Olive was undoubtedly Mother Chad's favourite sister and one year she was chosen to play Mary Queen of Scots which was a lavish play. My darling mother could not attend the school concerts in Ootacmund like she did as a guest of honour in Jubbulpore but as usual we were all in the concerts because all of us are good actresses. Mother Chad loved Olive's hair because she once had hair like Olive's. Thank God the barbaric custom of cutting a nun's hair off has almost gone out of fashion.

Easter was lavishly celebrated in Nazareth Convent. It began with a marvellous breakfast, I still remember the excellent food in this school especially the breakfasts because I was fascinated with the rosettes of butter every morning. The convent had its own farm, this school had everything. After breakfast we all raced into the beautiful woods which also had a lovely lake. I can still smell the pine trees, arum lilies, pansies, daisies and many other wild flowers. The staff had hidden the Easter eggs in the woods and we girls had to find them. I did not like to disturb the friendly butter cups and forget-me-nots as they popped up their heads to say 'hello' so I never found any Easter eggs, I was too busy talking to the flowers! But one year I did win the largest Easter egg in the world. I was standing beside Mother Chad when she raffled this enormous egg. I took note of the careful way she had folded the winning ticket consequently it was very easy for me to pull it out. My sparkling eyes have always been my greatest asset; they used to shine like diamonds when I was young but now when I get depressed they loose their magic and die.

I was always getting into trouble for saying little odes to my friends in lines and Mother Chad frequently caned me for my words of wisdom. When I was doing my Junior Cambridge at the age of fifteen she caned me unmercifully for talking on a walk. We convent girls were never allowed to walk in twos we always had to be three.

I wonder why? Anyway I began to chat because the walk to the school where we sat these exams was very long. When Mother Chad heard about this petty incident she sent for me to her famous study. She looked and acted like a demon. 'You have talked on a walk,' she said in rhyme. 'Put your hand out,' she said in a commanding voice.

After she had whacked me several times she put the cane in the corner and I foolishly said, 'Thank you,' in between sobs. She grabbed the cane again in a temper.

'I am going to teach you a lesson for being so impertinent,' she said and she gave me one more hard whack. This caning never taught me a lesson because I talk in queues at the till in Waitrose. I write books now in order to talk to people. Mother Chad left me in her study and she did not return until 10 pm and then she had only called in because she had left something on her desk. I was standing in the corner as stiff as a poker. She looked very shocked and ashamed of herself when she saw me standing in the dark in her study. I had not eaten for hours! She left her study and she brought in a sister who took me to the refectory where I was given a lovely meal at about 10.30 pm.

Our letters home were censored and she once asked me, 'Who's Mickey?' you seem to send him a lot of kisses.

I burst out crying, 'He is a dog,' I sadly exclaimed.

I left Nazareth Convent with two romantic memories the first one being a secret love affair between Mother Tony who was my Irish teacher and a Franciscan monk. Mother Tony was teaching us the Pythagoras theorem when Mother Chad walked into our classroom with a handsome Franciscan monk. I got excited because I always know when 'love is in the air'. Mother Tony blushed and she could not continue with the lesson but this kind monk came to her assistance and he carried on from where she left off. Poor Mother Tony was in a trance and her face was as red as a poppy! Nobody else detected the electricity between these two people but I did and when Mother Chad casually walked away with him after the lesson was over Mother Tony rushed after them. I got up from my desk to have a peep at her through the half open door, she pursued the chase for her lost love halfway down the corridor but then her vow of chastity made her turn back and she walked away with her head down deep in thought. Again I rebelled at another Catholic Church man-made dogma – the rule of celibacy!

When all the girls left the classroom I remained behind to talk to distressed Mother Tony. 'Who was that man?' I asked her frankly,

'He is not a man, but a monk my dear,' she said trying to fight back the tears.

'I know he's a monk but I also fell in love with him the minute I saw him,' I said trying to gain her confidence.

'Well he once asked my father for something but he refused so I became a Franciscan nun and be became a Franciscan monk. It's as simple as that.'

I gave her a hug and I left her alone with her thoughts. I understood all about love because at seven years old I fell madly in love with Monsignor Doubleman who was at least forty years older than me and at fifteen I could have easily fallen in love with Mother Tony's 'secret love'. I have been trying to find a father figure all my life but I get young men who are looking for a mother substitute and so the Oedipus complex goes on. These two men were vastly different from one another and if I had to make a final choice between them I now think I might choose the Franciscan monk in his simple robe and sandals because he was not disguised by magnificent regalia!

The second romantic memory occurred when I was sent to the boys' table in the refectory for talking in lines. As soon as I approached the boys they all began to smile from ear to ear and since I did not expect such a warm welcome I became shy. In order to break the ice a small boy stood up immediately and he offered me a chair. 'My name's Mr Fox,' he said shaking hands with me. 'What's yours?' he asked smartly.

'I'm Cheetah, the boy eater,' I replied quickly to match his wit.

All the boys began to clap and laugh. It was absolutely wonderful to have the attention of a dozen boys! But 'I only had eyes for one'. I liked Jack, the Maharaja of Mysore's son and I could not stop flirting with him. But I also liked Mr Fox.

'When I grow up I'd like to be in your harem, Jack,' I told him most sincerely and in return he gave me a Maharajas smile of approval.

Many years later I tried to flirt with the handsome Maharaja of Baroda at Firpos when he was dancing with his latest American girlfriend but he ignored me. Maharajas have been known to have women of every nationality but I do not think that they like to dance with Latins because they think that South American dancing is undignified!

I was sent back to the girls' table after three days in spite of the fact that my punishment was for a week. This unusual meeting with many boys gave me the confidence to handle men for life, they are only grown-up boys! I wonder what became of the little boy who acted like a perfect gentleman offering me a chair? I like to think that he became a doctor in order to help convent girls.

I remember talking to an interesting man at the check-out in Waitrose many years ago about Ooatacmund because I still talk in lines and he asked me, 'Are you from snooty Ooty?' in his best BBC accent. I replied, 'I'm not snooty, but I was in school in Ooty.'

In conclusion I must mention a very strange thing happened on my last night in Nazareth Convent, as usual it involves Mother Chad. She was giving a late lesson to a few girls when I accidentally pulled my bed making a little noise in the classroom below. Mother Chad came stamping up the stairs and she grabbed hold of me and biffed me hard across my face and her ring which some brides of Christ wear hurt my nose and the blood began to gush out like a fountain. Poor Sister Bianca was horrified when she saw the blood spurting out all over the place. She rushed me to a basin in the loo mumbling to herself as she tried to stop the bleeding.

It was on the last night in Nazareth Convent when I sobbed myself to sleep to the tune of 'Land of hope and glory' which was our end of term song I saw two ghosts they were nuns bending over my bed whispering, 'Shall we take her now?' asked one nun to the other.

'No. Not yet! Not yet,' was her reply.

I was not afraid of these ghosts they had lovely soft voices like sister Bianca. They both wore spectacles and I wanted to go away with them but I also wanted to go home to my beloved mother. But now I know the true meaning of this omen. I will write a book which will be published one day and my story will be told in the theatre, the cinema, the television and on the radio in every corner of the world. I remember Lawry's grandson taping my first book because he said that it would make a good 'book at bedtime'. When I saw him do this dirty trick I closed my book and I returned home in spite of the heavy rain and thunder. My physical and emotional suffering with loud ringing noises in my head, the pain of a trapped nerve and depression will be rewarded by God. I am a creative writer. I write about my own experiences of life. I am not a pseudo intellectual and God our Creator is the greatest artist and He knows all about human suffering and His will will be done. I do not really know if I will ever hit the jackpot, I have to wait and see, only time will tell.

Ode to Calcutta

Our new home was in Calcutta. My mother had sold 'Birdie House' in Mhow because Mary and Norine had left Nazareth Convent and Olive was about to leave as well which meant that Emerald and I would be going to a new hill school near Calcutta. Mother Chad actually wrote a good comment on my last school report, 'Nazareth Convent will miss Bridget who excelled herself at netball.'

My mother had returned to her mother's large house in Entally which was already overcrowded with her sister Alice – we called her Aunt Popsie – her husband, her three daughters and two sons. Then there was my mother, her five daughters and one son. Counting my grandmother and step grandfather we were sixteen people in the house! My mother introduced our much loved dog Mickey to the city life which he did not like at all. We all adored Mickey as he was part of our family and we begged our mother to bring him to Calcutta. The crowded atmosphere of two close families living in the same house with my grandmother was a short but very happy one. It was a temporary arrangement because my mother was going to rent a flat as soon as the Christmas holidays were over. She was going to move into an apartment with her three elder daughters. Mary and Norine had good secretarial jobs and Olive would be going to a Commercial school after Christmas which meant that my mother would be supported by her daughters. She did not like taking charity from her mother nor her rich sister Violet who had no children. My mother was a very proud lady and she found being a poor widow was very humiliating.

Calcutta is a town of great contrasts. There were the rich, both British and Indian, who had palatial houses in Ballygunge and Tollygunge which were on the outskirts of the city. There were also other nice houses and apartments in the town but most of the Burra Sahibs had their homes away from the bustling city. The poverty and squalor of many of the inhabitants in Calcutta is unbelievable. The beggars hang around Chowringhee like flies to a pot of honey. It was a common sight to see poor emaciated women carrying babies on their hips putting their frail hands out for a few pice. Many beggars lived on the streets and later when I grew up I always felt very sad to go into a fashionable restaurant like Firpos for a dinner dance with a boyfriend dressed in a glamorous gown having to fight my way through a sea of outstretched hands begging for money. I could not resist the children and I longed to take them all home with me and give them a bath and some good food and a clean bed for the night.

The most fascinating thing about Calcutta was the New Market where one can buy anything from a pin to a priceless

jewel! We had lived in the country so going to the New Market
was an adventure. The 'Maidens', or parks and green areas, were
well kept especially the grounds of the Victoria Memorial. The
business area was in Clive Street where we girls got good
secretarial jobs because we were well-educated. But during this
Christmas holiday we had a lot of fun with our cousins. We were
eight girls in the house and only three boys and they were too
young to play with us, but Aunt Nellie, my mother's eldest sister
had four grown up sons and after Mass on Sunday we often met
them at my grandmother's house, they were very handsome and
full of fun. I liked these cousins because they were terrible flirts,
like their mother and I enjoyed seeing the older cousins get on
well together. Convent girls are starved of boys' company and it
was nice to see my sisters and cousins go out to the cinema and
clubs with Aunt Nellie's sons. I was only fifteen so I enjoyed
being a spectator.

Sadly Mickey had not settled into his new environment and
my mother was very aware that she had made a mistake to bring
him to Calcutta so she took the necessary steps and sent him back
to Mhow with a railway guard to a friend's house. Everyone was
very upset giving my mother a very hard time and the anger
mixed with my tears must have been a terrible ordeal for her.

'Mummy is right,' I said trying to defend her. My mother was
always right and in the end we all kissed Mickey goodbye because
it was in his own interests to send him back to the country. This
exciting Christmas holiday flew past because we all had a good
family gathering due to our grandparents' generosity. I loved my
grandmother dearly because I could detect from the sad
expression on her face that she had had a terrible life with my
English grandfather. She bore him seven sons and five daughters.
All the sons, except one, died when they were babies and only
four daughters survived. My grandmother's father was Irish and
her mother was Dutch and she was totally unaware that her
English husband was a drunkard until she married him. But God
gave her a second chance and when her husband died from drink
she married a Mr A B Smith who had a good job in the
Telegraphs. We all owe a great debt to step grandfather Smith
because he saved my grandmother and her four daughters from

ruin. He was actually much younger than my grandmother and he married off all his step-daughters to Englishmen who had good jobs, all except my mother who wanted something spicier! My grandmother was a very shy lady and she hardly spoke to anyone but I adored her enchanting smile which spoke louder than her words. She, like all her daughters was a perfect lady but tragically her only surviving son committed suicide when he got into financial trouble leaving his little Irish wife heartbroken and broke. I was very sad when the time came to leave my grandmother's house but our Christmas holiday was over. Lynette and I had to say 'goodbye' to the bright lights of Calcutta and 'hello' to our new school in Kalimpong.

Ode to St Joseph's Convent, Kalimpong

Our new school was St Joseph's Convent in Kalimpong. As usual when the time came to go to school I was in floods of tears. I clung to my mother until the very last second as if I was never going to see her again.

'Goodbye, Mummy darling' I said kissing her with the tears rolling down my cheeks like rivers. 'I am going to miss you,' I sobbed.

As usual my mother kept her emotions under control. She had a very reserved English character and she always remained cool. The train journey was not as long as the journey to Ootacmund and my mother was right to change schools because Lynette and I would not have been able to undertake the long journey to Ooty alone because Calcutta was further than Mhow. The journey to Kalimpong became more interesting than the journey to Ootacmund when we changed trains at Siliguri and boarded the narrow gauge toy train to climb the foothills of the majestic Himalayas which is the greatest mountain range in the world. Lynette was reading so I sat alone gazing at the wonderful scenery which was more spectacular than the journey to the Nilgri Hills. The little toy train had to work harder, after all this was the home of the majestic Himalayas! As the train puffed along I got a glimpse of rosy-cheeked Tibetan women carrying their bonny babies on their backs picking tea. They smiled and waved at us and I waved back longing to have the babies in my arms. I had noticed that Tibetans had very weather-beaten but cheerful faces and wonderful smiles. They were sturdy individuals. The women wore their hair in long braids and I loved their colourful clothes. The men seemed very idle compared to the women who did most of the manual work, these women who carried our school trunks wore a padded head band which secured our heavy trunks on their bent backs.

It was very clear that the women did the 'donkey work' and the men hung around cheerfully smoking and talking with friends. Emerald and I had travelled with the school batch to Kalimpong in a comfortable second class compartment and we continued our journey with them until we arrived at Kalimpong. We boarded a bus at the station which took us to our new school. St Joseph's Convent could not be compared with Nazareth Convent because it was too isolated but Lynette and I soon settled down to our new environment. We had that certain polish which had rubbed off from Nazareth Convent and the nuns were delighted to have us and we were very popular with the girls. We had two princesses, they were the daughters of the Maharaja of Nepal we called them Cuckoo and Jean and their cousin's name was Tashi. These girls were friendly and intelligent and although they came from a royal family they never put on airs and graces.

I had very bad health in St Joseph's Convent in Kalimpong because of the altitude and bitter cold and looking out on the snow-capped mountains made me very depressed. I suffered from bad period pains which became worse and I had to take to bed every month with several hot water bottles in order to keep warm. I had another meaningful dream in this isolated convent which has haunted me for years! It was the feast of Our Lady of Dolors but because I was in terrible pain the nun in charge of the dormitory allowed me to lie in late so I did not attend Mass. I never knew that it was a feast day but I still remember the vivid dream as if it happened yesterday. In this mysterious dream I saw seven coronets floating down from heaven which signified the seven dollars. My mother, my four sisters and my brother all caught their coronets but when I tried to catch mine it floated away. I was trying to remember the third grace 'I will console them in their pains and I will accompany them in their work' the Virgin Mary promised. I awoke with a great sadness and I told the nun in charge of the dormitory about my dream.

'It is the feast of Our Lady of Dolors,' she told me 'Perhaps the Virgin Mary is trying to get in touch with you,' she said.

'Yes,' I replied. 'My dream has a deep meaning I feel sure of that,' I said pensively.

Perhaps my writing which I have been doing for my own enjoyment for many years was not good enough and I like to think that one day I will get my reward. An oyster has to go through a lot of suffering to produce one precious pearl and in the same way I have had several attempts at writing and now I have enough pearls to launch an unusual book.

A great tragedy happened when I was in St Joseph's Convent in Kalimpong which shattered my life for ever. It was the sudden death of my beloved mother. She went into hospital for a minor operation and three days later she died of renal failure. Lynette, who became a nurse in this hospital later found evidence that the famous gynaecologist who had delivered my mother of many of her babies had accidentally tied her ureters together. I believe her marvellous heart beat on until the bitter end in spite of the fact that her kidneys had ceased to function. I was heartbroken when Reverend Mother broke this bad news. Lynette took my mother's death bravely and so did my brother Claude who was in Goethalls' Memorial School in Kurseong but I broke down and cried because my whole world fell apart. Reverend Mother kindly allowed me to sleep in her room that lovely moonlit night but I could not sleep a wink because I kept running to the window banging on the glass and saying, 'Mummy, why didn't you ask me if you could have the operation? Why didn't you tell me about it in your last letter? Why? Why? Why?' I sobbed.

The tragedy of losing my mother when I was only sixteen years old made me more determined to find a husband to stand by me. Mothers can never be replaced. I had had a good mother but now I needed a man. I needed a shoulder to cry on someone strong who would take me in his arms and say, 'Darling, I love you. Darling, I will look after you.'

I needed a purpose for living. It is horrible being an orphan, it is worse than being a widow. I wrote my first book after my mother's death. It was actually a film script and I sent it to Helen Parish, a young actress and she in return sent me a lovely photograph of herself. I was only sixteen years old and at seventy-eight I still get enjoyment from writing. The only consolation about my mother's death was that she died on my father's birthday and I believe her last words were, 'Two men are standing beside the door in dress suits – they have come to take me away.'

I like to think that one man was my father and the other one was her father whom she adored in spite of his drink problem. My mother died in 1939 and that same year I remember Prime Minister Neville Chamberlain's dramatic speech on the radio.

'Great Britain is at war with Germany,' he said in his shaky voice.

We girls were all huddled together around the radio in the study hall. This war brought me great happiness and heartache!

Mary met Lynette and I at Howrah Station on our return from St Joseph's Convent, Kalimpong and I was just about to cry because I missed seeing my mother when to my great joy I saw Miss Taylor from Nazareth Convent standing there to greet me with her husband, she had got married. She had heard about my mother's death and she wanted to be at the station to meet me.

'My husband and I would like to adopt you,' she said jokingly.

She gave me a kiss and a hug and I walked away smiling with a very young attractive mother, Mary was only twenty-three years old!

Ode to St Helen's Convent, Kurseong

The war was gradually creeping into India because we began to see men from all parts of the world but I had to go back to school for another year because Mary who was now my mother figure decided to send me to St Helen's Convent in Kurseong in order to be near my brother who was in Goethalls' Memorial school. I had spent a very enjoyable Christmas holiday at rich Aunt Violet's house because when my mother died my sisters abandoned the idea of having a flat for the time being. It was a very frightening thought to be going to a new school with no sisters to fall back on. I did not want to leave Aunt Violet's luxurious apartment where we sat down to meals in an elegant dining room with a choice of menu on the table and return to a closed convent with refectories.

'Please let me leave school,' I begged Mary.

'You can if you become a nurse like Lynette,' was her blunt reply.

'But I don't want to be a nurse because I'm scared of dead bodies,' I told Mary.

'Well then it's back to school,' Mary replied firmly.

If I could have this choice again I would have become a nurse because death and dead bodies no longer frighten me. I would have had a career for life had I become a nurse because Lynette still does private nursing in America today, but above all I may have got a chance to marry a doctor who would have soon sorted out my ills with pills! I never got a second chance to change my mind so once again I was packed off to yet another school in the hills.

St Helen's Convent had a strange atmosphere something I had never experienced before. I was a new girl and I felt as if everyone was staring at me. I did not know it then that in this school everyone chose a 'special friend' for the school term and a couple of nights later when I was in the study hall a very popular girl with red-brown curls and brown almond eyes threw a little piece of paper to me. 'Will you be my "special friend"?' she wrote.

I happened to pick a pretty heart-shaped red flower which caught my eye that day after games and I threw this flower to her with my message tucked inside, it made a delightful envelope. 'Of course I'll be your friend' I wrote back.

And we both looked at one another and giggled. I definitely needed a friend, and a 'special friend' would be like a sister. I was missing Lynette and I needed someone to talk 'girl talk' with.

One day later on in the week when we were playing cricket or more to the point when I was talking on the cricket field instead of fielding, Sister Lydia, the drama mistress, sent a senior girl to tell me that Sister Lydia wanted to see me in her study. Sister Lydia was a romantic Russian Countess and I liked her the minute I met her because we had a good rapport. I left the cricket field immediately and I ran up the stairs to her study and I was breathless when I knocked on her door.

'Come in,' she said in a cheerful voice. As I came into the room she offered me a chair opposite her desk. 'Sit down my dear I want to talk to you,' she said softly.

I foolishly thought that she was cross with me like Mother Chad used to be so I burst out crying.

'Please don't cry, boys never cry,' she repeated over and over again.

'Have I done something wrong?' I asked impatiently.

'No, no my dear. I am just casting the characters for the school play and I want you to be the hero of the play so you must be as brave as a boy,' she said gently, handing me a tissue.

I smiled through my tears and she wiped them away with the tissue. 'The story is very interesting,' she continued. 'It is about a noblewoman who loses her son and she is trying to find him again. An impostor appears on the scene and he claims to be the rightful heir. But eventually a medallion accidentally falls from her manservant's neck which proves him to be her long lost son.

I have chosen you to be the noblewoman's son because you have very aristocratic features, I have also chosen your mother, the impostor, and your sister,' said delightful Sister Lydia clasping her hands together.

'Would you like to play this important young man?' she asked excitedly.

'Yes, if you think I can do it,' I replied humbly.

It was this play which involved four theatrical girls that eventually became a live drama! My mother in the play fell in love with me – was it an Oedipus affair? The son and impostor loved one another – were they homosexuals? And my sister also got a crush on me – was it incest? In other words we all got schoolgirl crushes on one another all due to romantic Sister Lydia! I had to rebuke my mother in the play most cruelly when she told me that she loved me and in return she wrote me a sublime letter on the proverb, 'To err is human, to forgive divine.'

I copied this beautiful letter and past it off as my own essay feeling dreadfully guilty. My relationship with the impostor was quite harmless just kissing and caressing, nothing more. But my poor sister in the play who was a tomboy was severely reprimanded in the study hall in public for writing a note to me which involved the word 'Darling... Please accept this camera from me as a parting present,' she wrote innocently.

All this young girl did was to make my bed for me when she got a chance to do it which was not often because I usually made my bed myself. Last but not least I was told off.

'I have written to your sister telling her that if you want to continue your studies it would be better for you to attend a day school because you have the power to instil love into the hearts of the most unlikely people,' she said sternly.

The power to instil love, I thought makes me out to be a witch. I love the song 'Witchcraft' and I have danced to it many times but I must try to banish this evil-minded nun from my memory forever. Headmistresses are a breed of their own.

I left St Helen's Convent at the age of seventeen only slightly awakened to my sexuality. It happened one day when a handsome young man came over from the seminary to give us a lesson on religion. He first drew a straight line horizontally on the blackboard and he wrote the word God and then he drew several vertical lines up to this line. Pointing to the horizontal line again he explained here is God and then he wrote the names of various religions on the vertical lines telling us that since all religions are trying to reach God all religions are true. 'People reach out to God through various channels,' he told us.

I have never forgotten this marvellous young man's explanation of his theory of God. I naturally fell in love with his brain and vision. We all believe that God is love and if everyone loves God we can then all love one another. In other words if human beings kept the first two commandments this world would be a beautiful peaceful and happy place. We can probably have 'heaven on earth' he told us. Sadly all human beings must die but our spirits can live for ever. I do not want to remember the toads in my life because I know that a toad can turn into a

Prince Charming and any girl can become a princess, if she behaves like a lady.

Ode to a Working Girl

School days were behind me now but the memory of those days still lingers on. When I left St Helen's Convent in Kurseong I took a six-month secretarial course at a private school instead of a nine-month one which Mary, Norine and Olive did at a Commercial College. I still do not know how I got away with it. Mary knew that I was a hard-working girl anxious to earn my own money in order to buy myself pretty clothes, shoes and handbags! I have always liked to look smart so I often borrowed Olive's dresses for school, sometimes with and sometimes without her permission. One day I forgot to change Olive's shoes which I had borrowed.

'You've got my shoes on,' she exclaimed in horror.

'Sorry, I forgot to change them,' I replied cheekily but Olive soon cooled down. It was this hunger for beautiful things which made me study hard and after six months I got my first job in Siemens (India) Ltd. Mr Greuter, the distinguished German Manager took me on as a junior secretary purely on my appearance! I must admit that I got all my jobs on that first impression but I kept them due to sheer hard work. I knew that I was not cut out to be a secretary because I could not master shorthand, it was Greek to me, but I was certain that I could write my own letters. I have to confess that on my first day at Siemens my wastepaper basket was full of torn up letters because they were not perfect enough for me. At the end of the day I broke down and cried but Mr Greuter who had great charm did not seem too concerned. My job at Siemens lasted nine months. We had to close down because we could not get our German products during the war. I was the first to be sacked because I was the youngest and the most incompetent. I only got eighty rupees a month and it was nice to get an extra month's salary because I was made redundant.

Mr Greuter was very sorry to give me my notice and I was equally sad to leave. I think he knew that I had a secret crush on him and when we shook hands before my departure I had to fight back my tears. But I was determined to find another job because it was when we were living in Ripon Street I saw what could easily happen to a woman who took up the oldest profession in the world! This poor creature's husband was a pimp and she had to work very long hours. She often came home dead drunk with her husband and a client and they played loud music while she worked. All pimps are toads and they should be exterminated.

My second job was in Mirlees Watson Limited. Mirlees Watson, like Siemens, was also an engineering firm and because I hate engineering jargon I had made up my mind to dislike the job. I worked for a little Scotsman but my English girlfriend worked for a tall handsome middle-aged bachelor, he was English and his name was Mr Longley. Mr Longley, like Mr Greuter, had great charm and because he was a bachelor I became infatuated with him. He was a perfect gentleman, I think he must have been at least forty-eight and I was only nineteen. Once again it was the older man who appealed to me because I was looking for a father figure. The little Scotsman was a toad but Mr Longley was a Prince Charming. I only worked in Mirlees Watson because Mr Longley called me in for dictation to give me a little confidence. He kept a fatherly eye on me because he knew that I found shorthand very difficult.

The Yanks had arrived in Calcutta and it was a great struggle to get to work every morning because quite often they would hold up the traffic and give me a wolf whistle and then stop their jeep in my path. I am a terrible flirt and I loved the adulation but winding my way around a jeep was tricky but great fun and no harm done except for one day when I was late for work.

'What's been the trouble, Ba? You're late,' said Mr Longley, trying to be serious. He called me Ba because I think that he compared me to a little lost sheep in a big city.

'It's the Americans, Mr Longley, they held up the traffic this morning,' I replied breathlessly.

'Are you sure it wasn't you Ba, who caused the traffic jam? You're a very pretty girl Ba, but you're asking for trouble by wearing too much paint on your face. Come here I'm going to take you up to my apartment to rub some of it off,' he said taking me by the hand like a child.

Mr Longley had an apartment above Mirlees Watson so we had to take the lift. His bachelor flat was tastefully furnished. He took me into the bathroom and he stood me in front of a mirror and he handed me a tissue. I gently patted some of the rouge off and I was dying to give him a kiss on his cheek to get rid of some of my lipstick. I think he read my thoughts and he backed away.

'Dab the lipstick off on the tissue as well,' he said evading my girlish giggle! When I think back on this all my Prince Charmings treated me like a child. However I did put on less make-up but it made no difference. When I was working in Mirlees Watson Mr Longley's secretary asked me out on a blind date with her Canadian boyfriend who was a pilot and this is when I met Aubrey Bond who was also a Hurricane fighter pilot. He was twenty-one and I was nineteen. I still liked Mr Longley but I dated the young pilot and quite soon 'Love was in the air'.

Sadly Mirlees Watson, like Siemens, had to close down because the firm could not get the necessary spare parts due to the war and I have no idea what happened to Mr Longley who has a very special place in my heart.

Ode to a Hurricane Fighter Pilot

All my sisters were gradually dating the Brylcreem boys and I was no exception. Lynette and I had had a brief crush on an Italian playboy who drove a very impressive flashy car but we both realised that he was a very shallow individual. When he used to call for Lynette at our flat in Ripon Street he always gave me a kiss behind the door before he walked out with her and I used to wave 'goodbye' to them from the window as they drove off. But when I met Aubrey I never bothered about this Latin from Calcutta preferring to go out with my handsome young Canadian fighter pilot. Aubrey Bond looked very much like Gregory Peck, he was tall and slim like him but his eyes were blue and not brown. His hair was fairer than Gregory Peck's and on the whole he was much better looking. We went out in a party when we first met and I soon realised that his pilot friends were very happy about Aubrey's new girlfriend. Previously he had been visiting a much older married woman who had a bad reputation. It was nice to see that his friends cared about Aubrey because he was only twenty-one and they kept an eye on him. He told me that he was engaged to a girl in Toronto. I still remember he mentioned that he lived in Yarmouth Road and later I discovered that he was a very experienced lover! I must admit that I wore very sexy clothes during the war but when I was young men respected girls. I was often asked what colour dress I would be wearing and matching orchids were lovingly pinned on to my dress by my many admirers. I now feel very guilty when I think about poor English girls of my age doing war work and during this same war I was being wined and dined in style. I always appealed to officers, not my choice but theirs.

I think that the song 'Hey there' describes me perfectly! I must have accidentally frightened the sergeants away.

Aubrey, like many of my boyfriends also spoilt me. He gave me a meaningful brooch of a Canadian maple leaf and a pair of silver wings as a lasting souvenir. I am ashamed to say I had so many silver wings in the end so I gave them all away to my brother's children. When I got married I destroyed all my love letters and I gave away all my souvenirs. I regret it bitterly today as I could have passed these treasures on to my own granddaughters and I could have told them a story about all the brave men I had met during the war. Flirts spread happiness and in a way I did spread a lot of happiness to many lonely men but now I am the lonely one living on memories! Aubrey was not a very good dancer because he was quite shy on the dance floor but I soon got rid of his shyness when we danced to 'If you knew Suzy!' which is a quick step. He and many of his pilot friends called me Suzy. They seemed to know that Aubrey was having a difficult time with me because unlike his previous married woman I was not prepared to go to bed with him. However 'fate' played a dirty trick on me one night when Mary had accidentally locked me out of our apartment in Theatre Road. Aubrey and I were sitting on the upstairs landing waiting for Mary to return home which gave Aubrey a chance to make love to me and I being very curious to know what was going to happen allowed him to kiss me. He fondled my breasts, kissed my ears, down my neck and at the same time he was skilfully putting his hand up my skirt. I wore camiknickers that night so I wondered how he was going to undo the three little buttons and if he did it clumsily I would have lost interest in the whole affair. But at twenty-one Aubrey was a marvellous lover, he knew all the erotic zones and when he placed his hand on my clitoris it was pure magic and before I knew what had happened I had experienced my first orgasm at the age of nineteen!

'Aubrey,' I whispered, 'please hold me close because I think I am going to die,' I sighed.

He held me tightly in his arms and asked me tenderly, 'Don't you know about masturbation, Suzy?'

'No, no I don't know anything because I have never allowed bad thoughts into my brain because it is a sin. I don't want to go to hell when I die,' I said sincerely.

'Petting' or masturbation was carried out by most young lovers when I was young because virginity was still a treasured possession. But I knew that every time I resorted to 'petting' I would have to confess this embarrassing sin to a priest in the confessional box. I never attempted to masturbate because I thought that only men had this mysterious power over women.

'Our love affair' like the song was a brief but very exciting one and sadly it came to a sudden end on Sunday, 5 December 1941. When the Japanese raided Calcutta Aubrey was shot down in his hurricane. His mates saw it happen, I believe he flew into the sun, blinding his vision and the Japanese pounced on his plane and shot it to bits. It is strange because at the exact time this tragedy happened I awoke with a start. I heard a big bang and I saw something burst into flames! It was a Sunday and I thought that I would be late for Mass. I believe in telepathy and omens, I even believe in fortune-tellers because some people have the power to see the future. I know that this book will make it to the top because I also know the future as well. Only time will tell!

Aubrey was going to take me to the cinema that Sunday night to see *The Meanest Man in the World,* and when he did not turn up I did think that he was mean because I was all dressed up waiting for him to arrive.

We never went dancing on Saturday night because his squadron had just moved to Calcutta and I thought that he would be tired. If only I had seen him and allowed him to spend the night with me like many lovers do now he might have been alive today, happily married to his fiancée! The Japanese got news of this move and they made their attack on Calcutta. I got the news of Aubrey's death on Monday morning when Norine phoned me at work. I believe Aubrey's uniform was found hanging up with two cinema tickets tucked into his breast pocket. His Squadron leader was trying desperately hard to contact me. I was working in the Deputy Director of Transportation's office and I almost had a nervous breakdown when I heard the tragic news as I could not stop crying.

'He was too young to die,' I told Norine over the telephone and the whole office saw my distress. My work in this office was all about movements of troops and squadrons and I typed many 'Secret' or 'Most Secret' letters daily for my boss who was a captain in the army. Olive worked for Brigadier Clutterbuck and once again it was a couple of Alberts sisters who helped the war effort in a small way. On the day of Aubrey's funeral I borrowed a black dress from Mary which was too tight for me and I bravely followed the gun carriage carrying a small bunch of red roses. The funeral was being videoed for his family but I knew that the coffin was too small because they only buried bits of him, the Air Force owed Aubery a decent-sized coffin but human life was cheap during the war. After the buglers sounded the last post and the rifleman fired a few shots in the air I walked up bravely towards the foot of his grave and I threw in my bunch of red roses. I grew up from a vivacious young girl into a young woman leaving a part of life's tragedies deeply buried with Aubrey.

Ode to an American Air Force Captain

It was Norine's American boyfriend who introduced me to Ted because after Aubrey's death I stayed at home and I listened to music. I had lost all interest in going out and Norine became very worried because I had lost my sparkle. It was Ted, again the older man, who gave me back my confidence. As soon as I was introduced to him I felt that I was in safe, experienced hands and before the night was out my vision of finding security and happiness was shattered. My sisters and I had decided to go to China Town in Calcutta for dinner with a party of Americans. I rarely went out with Americans because I had had a bad experience with a couple of American officers who took me in a party to a curfew dance one night. These two toads had been observing me all night.

'You don't smoke, you don't drink. What do you do?' I was asked bluntly.

'Nothing. I like dancing,' I replied innocently.

A curfew dance during the war continued until 5 a.m. and when the time came for these toads to drop me home they frightened me to death. As I tried to step out of their jeep they accelerated and drove off. This threatening behaviour continued for quite a while until I burst out crying and I was saved by a glorified whore who told them, 'Let her go, she isn't one of us.'

I owed my life to these glorified whores!

However at this moment of time I am writing about Ted who was a Prince Charming. He escorted me to his waiting taxi and when the Sikh taxi driver was weaving his way in and out of the horrific traffic in Chowringhee he was calmly serenading me with 'Moonlight becomes you'. He held both my fragile hands in his large capable ones. The bright tropical moon, his smart uniform and his mature handsome face made me fall head over heels in love with him by the time we arrived in China Town which is a maze of narrow streets. We had arranged to meet at the Chung-Wah Restaurant and when Ted and I arrived the others were waiting for us in one of the private dining rooms. As usual the conversation revolved around petty things so my thoughts drifted away but I soon woke up when I heard Mary ask Ted a frank question.

'Are you married?' she asked and Ted gave her an equally frank reply.

'Yes I am.' He then opened his wallet and carefully removed a piece of tissue paper and unwrapped it lovingly showing a lock of beautiful raven hair like mine. I had to admire Ted's honesty and I was flattered to think that I had the same hair as his wife. I glanced around the table and I caught another toad slyly taking his wedding ring off and slipping it into his wallet.

'You're also married,' I told this toad. 'I saw you slipping your wedding ring off,' and he ashamedly put it on again.

'My wife's name is Marie,' Ted continued which happens to be my second name. How strange I thought but I was too upset to comment. Fate was playing another dirty trick on me.

'I can't allow Bridget to get involved with a married man,' Mary told Ted quite firmly but he knew the whole story about Aubrey's death and I admired his braveness when he defended me.

'I'll walk out of Bridget's life when she's ready. Give me a week,' he pleaded 'I only want to help her to come to terms with the recent tragedy,' he added.

I took to bed for a week because I had had two love affairs go drastically wrong and during this week Ted brought me flowers, he filed my nails and he enjoyed brushing my hair. He did all the caring things he must have done with his wife. He finally said 'goodbye' to a laughing girl and I stood on the balcony and waved goodbye to him.

'Remember, if you ever need me you can contact me through The Bank of New York in New York,' he shouted as he waved back.

Many years later when I was in New York with my daughter Tessa I called into the Bank of New York and I tried to contact Ted but I was unable to do so.

Ironically Ted was the first but certainly not the last banker in my life. I appeal to bankers because I am like a cheque that will not bounce! All the bankers in my life have been Prince Charmings!

Ode to a Spitfire Pilot

Several memsahibs went to the hills for the summer and we sisters were no different. One year Mary decided to rent a cottage in Darjeeling where we spent a fortnight's holiday. It was a nice house, very similar to an old Victorian one.

It was good to have our freedom, because freedom for an ex-Convent girl was very precious indeed. We had spent a holiday at a guest house called 'Pekoe Tip' the previous year which was very well run by an English lady in Darjeeling. But this year Mary thought that it would be a nice change to rent a house so that we could entertain our friends.

During the day we rode horses, took long walks and played tennis, but the evenings were spent at the Gymkhana Club meeting friends or dancing the night away. Darjeeling was full of handsome men in uniform and we sisters had a choice of either the Army or the Air Force who were only too pleased to have our company. The memsahibs were often dull and boring – besides they were all married – but an unattached girl, especially if she was a celebrity, could play the field and have a jolly good holiday, something she could remember for the rest of her life. I had one such holiday which is still a happy memory.

Saturday nights at the Gymkhana Club were great fun because the live band got everyone on the dance floor when they played lovely wartime melodies. People who wanted to jive could do so to 'In the Mood' and anyone who wanted to snuggle up to a man in a nicely pressed uniform could get very romantic to 'As Time Goes By'. This meaningful song was played all over Calcutta and my sisters and I had danced to it many times at Princes in the Grand Hotel and the Winter Gardens where we danced under the stars as the man in the moon gazed down on us! There were the whores who hung around the balconies in the Grand Hotel waiting to pounce on an unattached man in the Winter Gardens but they never stood a chance against the 'Alberts Sisters' who were very much in demand. We had been singing professionally since 1940 and the men queued up for a dance because we were all very pretty girls. We appealed to men in uniforms fighting a war unlike the 'Spice Girls' who appeal to children!

We wore beautiful matching dresses when we became professional singers unlike the 'Spice Girls' who look like rag dolls! We won a talent contest at the Grand Hotel when we sang 'The Woodpeckers Song' with Ted Frangopolo's band and we became celebrities overnight. The men brought the roof down clapping loudly, cheering and whistling. I sometimes compare the loud noises in my head to this exciting talent contest.

'Who shall we give the cheque to?' asked the compère.

'To the little one in red,' they replied in unison, which was me. I'd borrowed Mary's lovely red taffeta dress she had worn for her first dance which showed off all my curves as I shook my hips 'seductively', not 'vulgarly' and flirted with the men. I declined to accept the cheque but gladly accepted a beautiful bunch of flowers. As we had become famous singers throughout India from our broadcasts, a couple of records and our live charity shows we were well-known in Darjeeling which was responsible for many holiday romances.

Since Aubrey's death I was not particularly interested in dancing with everybody at the Gymkhana Club but when the band played one of my many favourite tunes I did dance because I hated refusing someone a dance when the melody was good. The eager men would rush up to our table and if we refused them a dance they walked away looking very dejected. But one Saturday night when the band struck up 'Brazil' I actually searched for a partner and this is when I spied a Spitfire pilot and I dared him to ask me for a dance. I hypnotised him with my eyes because I saw Trinidad on his epaulettes! I evaded the other men except this pilot who knew exactly what I was up to. He smiled shyly as he approached me because he knew that I was dying to dance with him. I am not going to mention this airman's name except to say that he had a French surname.

He had a handsome face, a fair complexion, lovely brown eyes and hair and a charming smile. I have danced with people from all over the world but I had never danced with someone from Trinidad. 'Brazil' had the rhythm and we enjoyed ourselves so much that we never changed partners again.

My Spitfire pilot was on a weekend leave so we made the most of the night dancing long after my sisters had returned home. He dropped me back in the early hours of the morning in a romantic rickshaw. It was a glorious moonlit night and he had his arms around me all the way home. When we arrived at our cottage I ran up the hill daring him to chase me which he did several times. Every time he caught me he would clasp me in his arms and say, 'My nose is itching.' I knew that he wanted to kiss me but I would giggle like a school girl and break away. As we performed our 'Flirting ballet' Mount Everest and Kanchenjunga sent us flurries of snow kisses! We never did kiss that night but he turned up next morning to take me to Mass in another lovely rickshaw. As we journeyed in style we chatted happily which was when I discovered that he was engaged to a girl in Trinidad and this was why be behaved like a perfect gentleman 'on that lovely weekend'.

Many years later I met an assistant in a shoe shop in Weybridge who was also from Trinidad and she told me that she knew my Spitfire pilot and his family very well. He was living in England and he was still a pilot. She gave me his phone number and I rang him up one day and I left a message with his wife asking him to ring me back but perhaps his wife did not give him the message. I only wanted to recall a nice friendship not a passionate romance. .

Ode to a Blenheim Bomber Pilot

Norine was dating an Australian who was an observer in the RAAF who was anxious to come down more frequently from Akeyab to Calcutta to see her. He decided that it would be a good idea to introduce me to his pilot and I was only too pleased to meet him. I liked going out with the Australian airmen because they were different from the RAF, they were more down to earth. Walter, the Blenheim bomber pilot was a pleasant looking Australian, he was a tiny man, with blue eyes and a tanned complexion. Norine's Observer by comparison was tall, slim and very good-looking, he had nice blue eyes and fairish hair. He was not my cup of tea and although Walter was very plain I liked him much better. I found the Australian accent very difficult to understand and since Walter was much older than me I found it difficult to communicate with him. We went out in a foursome with Norine and Jim but I did notice that Walter went off on his own as soon as he brought me home. I often wondered whether he dropped into the whores' residential quarters in Karaya Road because he seemed to be a man of the world and I did not blame him for rushing away. He once told me quite frankly, 'Suzy,' he called me, 'I'd have to go back into the bush for a year before I tackled you.'

He did appreciate going out with me and he gave me two parting presents, a pair of RAAF silver wings and a delicate cultured pearl necklace. I could not believe that he was a Blenheim bomber pilot because he looked too tiny to fly these huge planes. In the course of the war I met many Australian airmen and one New Zealander. Jim was a spitfire pilot and he was shot down in the jungles of Burma. Jim always hailed a taxi rather than walk a few yards so I hate to think how he survived in a jungle.

I also remember meeting a handsome twenty-four-year-old Australian Air Gunner briefly, and I knew that he was too good-looking to live, it was written on his face: 'Whom the gods love die young!' This young man was shot down by the Japanese as well. Unfortunately the Burma Front was the forgotten war but I like to think that the 'Alberts Sisters' helped to keep the forces happy with their twice monthly songs on the radio and their many live performances.

Ode to the Senior Service

During the end of the war Olive and I worked for the Directorate General of Aircraft, it was our second and final attempt to help in the war effort and this is when I met the Senior Service. It happened one Sunday quite by chance when I cycled down to see Olive and her family. Olive married a boy born in India during the war, his father was Italian and his mother was English. She was entertaining her sister-in-law's husband and his Naval officer friend to a curry lunch when I turned up on my cycle. Sunday lunches in India consisted of curry and rice and all the spicy pickles washed down with pints of beer. I was feeling lonely that Sunday afternoon and had accidentally barged into what had been an interesting lunch party and I arrived just when the Naval Officers were about to leave, so Olive was obliged to introduce me.

'Murray, this is my sister Bridget,' she said introducing me to a very good looking Irish sub-lieutenant who had blond sun-bleached hair and twinkling turquoise eyes!

We shook hands and when our eyes met there was an immediate rapport.

'The boys are leaving,' said Olive who seemed very flustered.

'I'm sorry, I can see the party's over' I said breathlessly.

'No, it's nice to see you again,' said Olive's sister-in-law's husband. I had met Ivan several times but I never knew he had such an attractive bachelor friend. I like the Irish and I wanted to make a lasting impression on this young man. I did not want to get involved with the Navy because sailors have a girl in every port. When I went on board ship to a dance once every man told me the same thing,

'You look just like Hedy Lamarr,' which made me believe that this likeness was true!

My meeting with Murray was brief but I was not at all surprised when be phoned me the next day and neither did I know how he got my number.

'Would you like to go to a cinema tonight?' he asked me and I was delighted to accept.

'Yes I'd love to go,' I replied.

Murray called for me in his jeep and he took me to the Lighthouse cinema and we sat in the back row. When the lights dimmed Murray put his arms around me and he began kissing my ears, my neck, and my cheek. I did not want my lipstick smudged so I turned my face away. I had never been made love to in a cinema and I really did think that the Senior Service worked fast but apart from the fact that he was kissing me in a public place I enjoyed the attention. I could not resist him because he was very handsome. When the cinema lights came on again he stopped kissing me but the moment they went off we behaved like a couple of teenagers although we were both twenty-one. Murray gave me a pretty pair of 22 carat gold earrings, they were little shamrocks and I adored them.

Murray was in Calcutta for a few weeks and he took me out every night. He arrived late for a dinner date at Firpos one night and I noticed that he paid the bill with a wallet full of wet notes telling me that he had fallen into the river! 'Could my handsome Irish Navel Officer be a drunkard?' I queried. I knew what a tragic life my grandmother had with her drunk husband. How can one fall into a river unless one was drunk? But when one is young and in love or infatuated with a person one tends to turn a blind eye to all the little tell-tail signs that become larger than life later on. I tend to look at people through rose tinted spectacles. In my eyes Murray was not a toad, he was a Prince Charming!

It was at Princes when we were dancing one night under the crystal ball like many young lovers I got a glimpse of ourselves in the mirrored pillars on the dance floor. Murray with his sun-bleached blond hair and turquoise eyes, and I with my raven hair and hazel eyes made the song 'Night and Day' seem as if it was written for us. I now compare depression to a long dark tunnel in the night and I long for a sunny day! It never goes away completely in spite of what people say. It is a cruel illness that has no beginning or end. I was born an emotional person and I have always needed a mature man to stand by me. Instead I got the boys who have their fun and then ran away. Meanwhile, for the next couple of months Murray sailed in and out of my life as his ship called at many interesting ports. He bought me beautiful silk to make a dress but when our love affair ended I sent this gift to a girlfriend in England because her need was greater than mine. But my 'dersie', or tailor, did make the lovely piece of cream woollen material into a smart blazer.

Our last few days together was at Christmas and this was when Murray asked me to marry him and I foolishly agreed. He took me shopping to the New Market in his jeep and I deliberately wandered down the jewellery shops to test his reaction.

An engagement ring was not something one got from a Christmas cracker, neither was it a sentimental thing but a serious commitment. I wanted to wear my ring proudly in order to keep the toads away. I had found my Prince Charming and I was prepared to settle down. Murray bought me a five diamond ring and he slipped it on my finger in the shop. We walked out of the New Market and he drove me home in his jeep. It was our last night together and Murray made love to me very tenderly though I spoilt it all by crying. Tears during love making can put any man off so we did not have a passionate relationship.

'I'm prepared to wait until we get married. I'll send for you soon darling,' he told me so honestly.

We had had an exciting day at the races that last week and I had lost a lot of money which was a bad omen because I am a very lucky person. I thought that I was losing Murray forever on that last night so my tears flowed like rivers. In the end we said 'goodbye' to one another in the early hours of the morning. After work that day I went to the New Market and I bought some wool in order to knit Murray a pullover. I sat and knitted diligently every day after work looking at my sparkling diamonds which seemed to be saying, 'I love you! I love you! I love you!'

Murray had written me several long romantic love letters from board ship but when he arrived in Ireland he stopped writing. I had finished knitting one pullover and I began knitting a second one and when that was completed I started on the third, patiently waiting for Murray's letter from Ireland. It took him fifty-six days to pluck up the courage to tell me that our engagement was off because he had to go back to college in order to work in the family business.

He told me that he still loved me and he wanted me to keep the ring. I never replied to this letter but I wrote to his brother in Belfast instead and I told him to tell Murray that I had received his letter. I tore up his portrait then stuck it together, looked at his face for the last time and destroyed it again into tiny pieces. I cannot call Murray a toad because when I met him he was a Prince Charming. Perhaps we both 'fell in love with love' which is make believe.

Ode to the Great Calcutta Killing

I was working for the chairman of the Chinese Supply Commission when the Mohammedans and Hindus began to slaughter one another which was a very frightening experience. We girls had to pick our way to work in order not to stumble over dead bodies lying in the streets and some were stuffed down the manholes. These riots flared up anywhere and at anytime and sometimes they continued from morning till dusk. Fortunately we girls felt very safe in our flat in Theatre Road because a couple of Indian Naval Officers lived above and they had guns which they told us they would not hesitate to use. Fortunately my brother's squadron was also posted to Calcutta during this violent period and he provided us with some tinned food because our servants were too afraid to go out. My feelings in this unnecessary slaughter were neutral because I had been brought up from a child with Mohammedan and Hindu servants who worked side by side in our home. In the army there had been differences between the soldiers because of their religious beliefs but individual quarrels never took place in a home or a street. It was unbelievable that when peace was declared India had to begin a civil war and we girls got caught up in it as well. I had to admire the guts of the people who sometimes defended their homes and themselves with nothing but a bamboo and some of them were quite elderly.

I often peeped at the chaos and confusion from my bedroom window and when an alarm was raised everyone came out to fight including the small children as well. I had always known Indians to be gentle, passive people but during the Great Calcutta Killing they turned into savages. The police force did a great job keeping the rival parties apart and on the whole things could have been much worse. Murray was chased by a few over-excited hooligans in Bombay but he sailed away leaving me behind to face this troubled time alone.

We had to have clean clothes for the office but our poor Dhobi (washerman) was a Muslim and he washed our clothes in a Hindu area. I decided to take matters into my own hands one day and I asked one of the Chinese employees to drive my Dhobi and I into the Hindu area to recover our clothes and he was very brave to undertake this dangerous job. I thought that his military uniform would scare the Indians and I sat in the front of the jeep beside him and my poor Dhobi disguised as a woman sat at the back. However, we suddenly came into a densely populated area and the people crowded around the jeep eyeing my Dhobi suspiciously. I gave the Chinese driver an immediate order to make a swift turn in the middle of the road and head for home. My father would have been proud of this quick manoeuvre because we were heading for trouble. The Chinese Supply Commission was financed by the Americans because they were supporting General Chiang Kaishek during the war and I worked for Mr Sherman Wong who was educated at Harvard University. It was the best job I ever had because the Chairman and I did no work!

I remember asking him one day, 'Why do you keep me as your secretary, Mr Wong, because I don't do any work?' and he gave me an enchanting reply.

'In China it is a custom to have a flower in the office, *you* are that flower,' he said smiling at me.

Mr Wong was a perfect gentleman and he had an aura of serenity about him. He sat at his palatial desk and chain-smoked all day and 'The Great Calcutta Killing' did not harm a hair of his head. I often wish I could be as calm and composed as the Chinese because one day I am sure that China will become the greatest world power and nobody will know when it happened!

India's independence arrived at last basically due to Mr Ghandi's non violent protests. Mr Ghandi was a great man; he fought for freedom in a very diplomatic way.

Ode to India's Independence

My father told my mother many years ago: 'Annie, there will come a day when our children will work for Indians. The Indians will become the employers and our children will be their employees' were his words of wisdom. My father was already working for an Indian and Prime Minister Sharmsundalam was a very mean man. My father made the forests of the Holkar State pay their way, he did a very difficult job and because of the stress and worry he died at the age of forty-two of a stroke. The rich Holkar State gave my poor widowed mother pittance for a pension and a paltry sum for each child until the age of eighteen which was a disgrace. My father was a brilliant man he had to learn how to read and write in Hindi before he got the job of a Forest Officer in the rich Holkar State.

He often told my mother that working for an Indian prime minister was 'blood earned' money and his hard-earned money did last my mother a lifetime. In the same way I feel that writing a book, no matter how short the story is, is also blood-earned money – this is definitely my last attempt! Previously I never bothered to get my work published but now I am determined to write a meaningful book, something my children and grandchildren can be proud of. Like my father, I am a woman of words and deeds.

The Chinese Supply Commission had closed down and once again I was out of a job so I moved on to The Aluminium Manufacturing Company. I became the private secretary of the biggest toad in the world. My boss should be called King Toad because he hired me then fired me for nothing. I shared his private office for a few weeks when he offered me an apartment in a posh residential area. I innocently saw the apartment and I liked it.

'Can I have my sister living with me?' I asked him frankly.

'No, I'm afraid not. If you do take the apartment only I will have another key because I might have to call on you from time to time to see if everything is in order,' he said sheepishly.

'If I cannot have my sister living with me I don't want the apartment,' I replied and that statement was just the beginning of this toad's venom.

He turned me out of his office and I was told to do the filing, a very humiliating job for an experienced secretary. I am glad I took up this mammoth task because I renewed the entire filing system in The Aluminium Manufacturing Company which was in terrible disorder.

During this period of unrest the Indians were clamouring for their independence and King Toad was shaking in his shoes because the factory workers began to strike and vent their anger personally at him, on many occasions. This was much to my glee because I despised this toad of Calcutta who should have been in the gutter. But I continued to do my job silently for him. One day when I received my salary at five minutes to one o'clock I asked Mr Toad's permission if I could put it in the bank which was just across the road. I always put cash straight into the bank as soon as I get it.

'No,' he replied. 'You can wait and put it in during your lunch hour.'

I would have accepted this reasonable solution had he not threatened me. 'If you put your money in now you'll get the sack,' he told me.

But he would have to give me one month's salary as

compensation, I thought, so I dared to go to the bank.

As toad had said, an envelope with a large amount of notes was waiting for me on my desk when I returned with a short note:

Dear Miss Alberts

Your services are terminated as from today. Enclosed please find one month's salary in lieu of notice.

I picked up the money and I walked out.

'Goodbye everybody,' I said cheerfully 'I'm going back to the bank again.'

Everyone laughed because I have always been popular in my many jobs.

When I walked into the bustling streets the tears rolled down my cheeks like rivers! I had no job and no apartment, only a tiny room in the YWCA in Middleton Row. In India we do not have national assistance when one is out of work so I quickly dried my tears and walked on bravely into a girlfriend's office. I usually went to see my friends or my sisters during my lunch hour and this is how I got another job, I had to be seen to make the new office keen to employ me! My friend was working in KLM and I got a job in Java Bengal Line which was a Dutch shipping line. They needed an assistant who could do her own correspondence because she had to run the shipping and air department independently. Mr Beales, a kind Dutchman interviewed me for the job and he tested me on a few general knowledge questions. I used to call at KLM and Java Bengal Line's office quite regularly so it was no surprise when Mr Beales offered me a job. I liked the smart uniform which was similar to the KLM air hostesses. I had to work at the counter, booking sea passages on two luxury liners the *Oranje* and the *William Ruys* and I also booked passengers by air on KLM. I had to deal with our cargo boats which took a few passengers as well. Since Mary and her husband, who was another toad, were on their way to England I booked them a passage on one of my cargo boats because they were marvellous value. The food was excellent and since these boats called at many ports en route the passengers were able to see many interesting places. I knew that Mary would love the long sea voyage and her husband who was a ravenous toad would enjoy the food!

Mary and her husband were lucky to be leaving India, leaving poor Norine and I in the YWCA. Mary had sold all the furniture in our apartment in Theatre Road to a new tenant and, because the anti-British feeling was spreading, she thought that Norine and I would be safer in the YWCA. One day when I was walking in Clive Street I was approached by a gang of youths.

'Wear a sari or go back to England,' I was told aggressively. If I had my way I would wear a sari in England because they are very beautiful but they only suit Indian women who are very graceful creatures. During the fight for independence Clive Street became the main target because it was the business area and many British businesses were closing down. The factories were also badly hit and the constant strikes made many of them close down and this is when King Toad came running to me to get him back to the U.K. I could not believe my eyes when I saw him across the counter looking as frightened as a pussy cat.

'Can you book me an urgent passage on one of your boats, Miss Alberts?' he asked.

'Certainly,' I replied, trying desperately hard not to laugh.

I booked him a passage on either the *Oranje* or the *William Ruys*, this booking was made fifty-one years ago!

When Indonesia wanted their independence our office had to lock all doors and windows in case we were attacked, it was quite frightening but I am a survivor because in spite of my problems I am still on this planet to tell the tales.

Ode to Mr Ghandi

Yesterday, Tessa and Gerald kindly invited me over to 'The White House' to see a marvellous video of Mr Ghandi's life. What an incredibly brave character this great man had. If he was a Catholic, I am certain that the Pope would have canonised him on his death. I do not care if Mr Ghandi is a saint or not but I am

certainly going to ask him for guidance. We are both peaceful
people because I believe in 'non violence', it is better than war. I
am sure if Mr Ghandi was still alive he would have solved all the
recent wars we have been having all over the world.

It is ironical that when Mr Ghandi was treated violently he
resorted to spinning cloth in order to make his simple clothes. I
am also spinning words together to help me to come to terms
with life. The most charming part of the film was the marriage
vows which Ghandi and his wife repeated one after the other.
They were both only thirteen years old. They took seven steps
and made a vow on each step, the words were beautiful and their
marriage lasted a lifetime.

It seems that seven is a symbolic number. I saw seven objects
in a room which prompted me to write a book. I also had a
religious dream about the Virgin Mary sending seven coronets
from heaven but I never got one. I hope that on the completion of
this book I shall get my reward. I was only fifteen years old when
I had this dream and it may happen sixty three years later.

Ode to Che Sara Sara
(Or Ode to What Will Be Will Be)

Richard and I had a strange meeting. He was a Bryanston boy
educated in a public school which was known for its liberal
outlook on life and I, on the other hand, am a boarding school
convent-educated girl. We met at a dance and we had a steady
eighteen-month courtship which was full of fun. However, fate,
life, or God decided that we were made for each other and what
was a peaceful affair turned into a nightmare when I found that I
was pregnant. We had a strong bond between us but both of us
were not prepared to have a 'shot gun' marriage. But since I had
been to see the Parish priest neither was I prepared to have an
abortion. I thought a sensible compromise would be for us to
marry in the registry office.

I would never have got in touch with Richard again if it had not been for one of Richard's friends, he was a sensible mature man and he was able to reason with me.

'Richard really loves you, Bridget, but he is afraid that he will never be able to support you,' he told me most sincerely.

'That's fine. I am going to support myself and my baby,' I replied confidently. But Syd was determined that the wedding should take place and he told me that he was going to be Richard's best man. This wedding cost me a lot of money because I paid for Richard's hand-made wedding suit which was a disaster! I also bought my own wedding ring and a signet ring for Richard as well. I bought my beautiful wedding dress which was also hand-made and Norine's pretty georgette dress and hat to match. Norine looked exquisite in salmon pink which contrasted with my blue chiffon and lace dress. Norine was my bridesmaid, and Tessa was my flower girl! My wedding day was the only day I had not been sick. My little cherub was happy because she had chosen her own parents. I also bought my own three-tier mini wedding cake and a bottle of champagne suddenly appeared. I think Syd bought it. We were only five people at the reception in Richard's apartment including the registrar, and then we went to a dinner dance at Princes.

Richard had a high temperature the night before our wedding day. It was a nasty attack of malaria which troubled him from time to time and he looked thoroughly washed out. I also had second thoughts as to whether I was doing the right thing to marry Richard. I lay in bed late on my wedding morning in the YWCA watching my beautiful wedding dress twist and twirl as if it was poking fun at me. 'Your dancing days are over! No more flirting and no more boyfriends on a string. The string must be cut into tiny pieces and burnt,' said my dress dancing about under the fan. I knew that a 'shot gun' marriage was not the solution. If I had my life all over again I might have kept Richard as a partner.

I would have moved out of the YWCA into Richard's apartment. I would have been able to show Richard what an excellent housekeeper I am. In Nazareth Convent we girls were taught how to manage our staff and I was the best in the class for allocating what job had to be done by who.

Perhaps one day I shall have the guts to put an advert in *The Times*.

Lady, seventy-eight years young wishes to become a housekeeper
in a stately home. Any offers?
Phone number 007.

I will put this advert in for fun and see if I get any replies.
Knowing my luck I am certain that I will get many replies with a
telephone number like 007. As usual I have to have the number
seven which happens to be my lucky number and James Bond's as
well!

We did not have to go to the registry officer to get married
because the registrar came to Richard's apartment. During the
ceremony Richard and I made our wedding vows but since it was
not a church wedding they meant nothing to me. It takes two to
tango, two to marry but it takes more than two to *love*! It takes
three or four or may be more – it takes *time*! Richard and I did not
base our marriage on sex alone because we grew to love one
another as friends. Sex in my opinion often ends a relationship
especially with someone like me. I should be called ——frigid,
rigid, Bridget! I am not a bit like Bridget Jones. My book is going
to be different to *Bridget Jones' Diary*. My story is going to be far
better than hers, *The Graduate* and *The Summer of 1942*.

My book is going to bring back moonlight, music and
romance! Everyone is tired of modern sexy films, it has become
boring. We need a change, we want everyone, including the
young and old to have a lot of fun and no harm done. I want the
world to dance!

My left leg is getting lame but I try to keep it mobile by
putting on music every day and I dance by myself. I have lost
Richard who was my dancing partner but when I go to heaven I
would like to have one dance with Fred Astair to a haunting
melody called 'Dancing in the Dark.'

God says that in His house there are many mansions. I want to
be sure that God puts me in His ballroom when I die so that I can
dance with all my old boyfriends and Richard again. This
morning I woke up singing 'It's June in January' when I took my
shower. I telephoned my best friend June and we ended up
singing this song together. This same song was rambling about in
my head in 1994 when I was writing 'Swan Songs'. I would like to
dedicate this song to June. Music seems to be gradually creeping

around in my brain for several weeks now. Music is essential to our family because all of us still love music and none of us would like to live in a world without music and dancing.

I would like to think that my book will be made into a musical and that it will be enjoyed by everyone.

This last attempt at writing my musical autobiography would never have happened because my consultant psychiatrist for the elderly had decided to knock the ringing noise out of my head by giving me a medication which is used for schizophrenia in order to knock out the voices. Joan of Arc also heard voices and yet she was a saint! I wonder what medication psychiatrists would have given her? All consultants are very special people, a doctor does not become a consultant overnight and my present consultant stepped in when psychiatrists had given up on me.

It is important to remember that doctors take the Hippocratic oath so they must try to help a patient who comes to them when previous treatment has not worked.

My brave consultant has taken me on knowing that I have been in psychiatric care for twenty-eight years.

Is he a terrorist or a Prince Charming? He is neither, because he is a good doctor, his conscience told him to help me. Since he is a consultant who specializes on the thyroid gland I had no alternative but to seek his help. Fortunately I had a delightful foreign lady doctor once who was my GP and she sent me to this consultant many years ago. I will not let him down because his reputation is at stake. He has captured my personality; I am not difficult to understand but I must keep my personality until I die. I am a mother figure to everyone. I have only had two children but I have mothered many foreign children from all parts of the world for years. I need to have young people in my life but I do not wish to substitute real live children for books! Writing a book is a very solitary occupation, fortunately I come alive when my lodgers return home. Some women write books because they have the urge to create, there may be some truth in it because at the moment I am eating like a horse and getting as fat as a pig. I did this over-eating when I was pregnant. I was a tiny girl weighing about 9 stone but when I was having a baby I ended up weighing 11 stone 4 lbs! My blood pressure was double the normal range. I did not want Tessa to be labelled 'illegitimate' so I refused to be induced. Colonel Fisher showed Richard and I the X-Ray. Tessa had unravelled herself from the normal foetus position and if I had a normal labour she would have broken her neck and both of us would have died.

Richard was instructed to take me to the Elgin Nursing Home that evening. As usual I broke down and cried and for the first time in my life I saw tears in Richard's eyes as well. He was afraid that he was going to lose his 'Petsywee' and neither did I want to leave my 'Hubba'.

As we were driving to the Elgin Nursing Home we drove past the Catholic church and I begged Richard to stop. 'Why? For God's sake why?' he asked.

'Because I want to get married in the Catholic Church. I want to go to heaven when I die,' I replied in between sobs.

'But we are already married,' he said angrily. 'No we are not in the eyes of the church, I am living in sin,' I told him truthfully.

Richard was furious, he almost drove into a brick wall because he was in an awful temper but he stopped at the church in the end. The Parish priest greeted me and I asked him to marry Richard and I. 'Do you have a witness?' asked the priest. Just then I saw a marlie (gardener) putting a bunch of flowers on the altar and I called him.

'Yes we have one,' I said anxiously. 'Marlie, marlie' I beckoned. The poor little man was baffled by my strange request but he came running over to be our witness. Richard swore throughout the ceremony telling the priest that we were already married. When it came to putting my wedding ring on I realised that I could not get it off because my hands were very swollen.

I have done everything back to front in my life and my church wedding was just one more mistake. My life has been a 'Comedy of Errors' but I know that it will end happily. Richard has left some wonderful cartoons which I shall place at the end of this book. It is not going to be 'my book' it is going to be 'our book'.

Tessa and Simon are very lucky to have two talented parents who have left them a legacy of love in its truest form!

After my church wedding I went into the Elgin Nursing Home. I had nothing to worry about because Mary Ayah – who had been my eldest sister Mary's Ayah – settled everything in my room and she drove home with Richard to await Tessa's arrival. I waved goodbye to both of them and then I broke down and cried because it suddenly dawned on me that I was about to be a real mother at last! I have always adored babies and I practically brought up a cousin's daughter. I loved taking Victoria home with me on weekends and I would give her a bath and also buy her a few clothes. Her mother and two elder sisters were known as 'The Hudson Sisters' during the war, these cousins were professional singers and they travelled throughout India and Burma entertaining the forces. We sisters had jobs. Victoria needed a mother and I was only too happy to look after her sometimes. My cousin's mother was my father's sister Mary hence the name Mary and Claude continue in my family today.

I remember a nurse called Hilary prepared me for the operation that night. She appeared to know Richard she gave me a nice compliment. 'I have never met you before but I can see why Richard married you, you're so beautiful!' she said smiling at me. Preparation for a caesarean in 1950 is very different to what it is like now. Surgeons take care to give one a neat bikini scar but in my day we had a huge scar from the navel running down the centre of one's abdomen. I have had the same scar opened out three times but it has healed very well. But now my body has been mutilated by a barbarian who was supposed to be a plastic surgeon. The idiot was supposed to give me a tiny tummy tuck in order to get rid of some loose flesh and birth lines but he never looked at the skin. He added to my misery by giving me three huge scars. I am convinced that plastic surgeons cause more trouble than good. I do not know why young women go in for silicone boobs it is most unnatural.

Fortunately I still have good breasts but apart from them I seem to be falling to pieces but I will survive!

I vividly remember being carried downstairs to the theatre by four little men skilfully twisting and turning the stretcher under my instructions. 'Please don't drop me,' I told them several times on this precarious journey. I was relieved when I saw Colonel Fisher waiting in the theatre. He was grinning and I could not recognise him at first because he had removed his false teeth, a precaution all surgeons must take in case they fall into a patient's abdomen! I remember him bending over me and I put my arms around his neck and I gave him a kiss!

I did not like the chloroform and I fought it for a while and then I must have been knocked out. I woke up hours later surrounded by a group of medical staff who seemed to be concerned but Colonel Fisher calmed them all down. 'She's all right, she'll be okay,' he said. Later that evening Tessa was brought to me by a nurse smelling of chloroform. Richard was intrigued with her and commented, 'Doesn't she look like a Chinese idol?' and I smiled that silly remark away. Norine was also visiting me and Richard opened a bottle of champagne to celebrate Tessa's arrival. I am convinced that having a baby by a caesarean section is the easy way out because I had no labour pains or waters breaking etc. In my opinion it is a very civilized way of having a baby. Tessa's last baby Emma was also a caesarean but one cannot see her scar. Thank God surgeons behave like human beings now and not like butchers! Women must fight to keep their identities. We are not only 'baby machines!' I fought to keep my physical appearance when I was young but now I am fighting to keep the only precious gift I have left – my *personality.* I shall go down fighting for the right to be treated like an individual. I will choose to make my life worthwhile until the bitter end.

Today is 27 November, it is cold, bleak and black but for me it is 4 April 1950 and the weather is 104 degrees and I am over the moon with happiness! What a wonderful computer the brain is and to think that my beautiful brain had been knocked out by over medication of the thyroid gland. My consultant in London had a theory – if a doctor pumps the thyroid gland a patient can be kept sexually active more or less forever. Again sex is the 'be all and end all' of everything. The 1970s will go down in history as the 'Sex Revolution' similar to 'The Industrial Revolution' but the year 2000 is just the beginning of 'The Romantic Revolution'. Fashions change but in doing so they often revert back and I predict that romance is going to be back. One day we will look at the 1970s and compare them to the downfall of the British Empire. It was 'The Gay Revolution' which was the downfall of the Roman Empire!

To be back in India in my thoughts is magical. I left The Elgin Nursing Home in five days because I had a host of servants waiting for me in our apartment which was above Whiteaways in Chowinglee. Richard rented it for six months from an English couple who were going on leave, I had two nannies for Tessa. Mary Ayah during the day and Mrs Gomez, a Portuguese nanny at night. I also had a cook, and a bearer (butler) and a Metha (sweeper). They all had their jobs and a dhobi (laundry man) called once a week to pick up all the dirty clothes and return them beautifully washed and pressed a week later. Life in India for a married woman was sheer bliss. My occupation was still going out with Richard and friends but I had to obey certain rules! I came out of the nursing home on the fifth day which was too soon and I got a dreadful tummy upset which had an effect on Tessa as well. I was given a course of antibiotics which cleared up the infection but little Tessa had also brought up thick white mucus which smothered her face. Mrs Gomez arrived on duty at 4 p.m. and she was most concerned 'Madam! What has happened to baby's face?' she exclaimed.

And I burst out laughing because Tessa loved sleeping on her tummy and consequently she was smothered in a creamy substance. 'I don't know nanny,' I told her making it into a joke which did not go down too well.

Another amusing incident happened when Richard took me dancing in a party to Princes and I had to come home because I began to leak warm milk which ruined one of my favourite dresses. I was met in the hall by Mrs Gomez who was marching to and fro rocking Tessa in her arms. 'Madam! Poor baby has been crying!' she scolded me. 'She is hungry,' she said.

'I know but I came home as soon as my milk was ruining my dress,' I replied like an irresponsible teenager. But Mrs Gomez was not at all pleased. I nursed Tessa and I changed my dress and I went back to Princes. Ironically I had to throw away that favourite dress because the dry cleaners could not get the stain off which was my punishment!

Ode to Home Leave

It was very exciting for me to travel on the 'Strathmore'. We had a first class cabin deluxe with a private bathroom. I was fascinated with the voyage but long sea voyages do not agree with me because I get seasick and too much sea and sky depresses me. I do not like travelling by air either but I love trains and one day I would like to go on the Orient Express like Tessa and Gerald did. It was very interesting going through the Suez Canal which I thought was a marvellous Anglo/French achievement. The conjurors performed some marvellous puzzling tricks for the children when we docked at Aden and Tessa was captivated by them. The adults enjoyed them as well. Richard bought me a lovely string of pearls with earrings to match. The goods were excellent value but one had to bargain with the clever salesmen.

It was a very colourful sight to see the tiny boats come alongside our ocean liner holding up attractive things for sale. The duty free shop on board ship was also good value. Richard bought himself two colourful swimming trunks and Tessa kept an eye on the dry one until he needed it. It was delightful to watch her guarding her Daddy's swimming trunks and the only day we insisted that she should go to the nursery with the other children somebody robbed one of the swimming trunks! Tessa was not happy in the nursery and in the end we decided that it was better for her to be with us. Richard adored Tessa and they played many games together on deck and I was happy to see the strong bond between them.

There was a fancy dress party for the children and I was determined to send Tessa as Lady Godiva. I asked a steward for some hemp which I combed out carefully and I made Tessa a lovely long flaxen wig. Richard made her a horse out of a piece of wood.

I made sure she wore pale pink silk panties to be modest and she literally ran away with the 1st prize as the most original contestant. She delighted the spectators by peeping through her wig as she walked round the deck with her daddy's hand-made horse! Most of the children had costumes specially made for this show and our eighteen month old daughter stole the prize. We were very proud of her and so were the spectators.

The ship had a lot of entertainment for the passengers and Richard and I enjoyed the dinner dances. The live band was good which played lovely romantic songs. They also played South American music as well so Richard and I showed everyone our talent at dancing which was great fun. The twenty-one day voyage was too long as apart from swimming or playing bridge during the day I got bored with the sea and sky.

I disliked the arguments that went on after bridge in the 1st class lounge which made me make up my mind never to learn how to play this argumentative card game. I may take it up if I live to be ninety because I believe bridge is good for the brain. Most unlikely, because bridge seems to be a form of communication the elderly indulge in when they are getting senile! I would like to play whist which will be far easier because I shall be able to talk as well. I hate concentrating on anything. I write my books straight off the cuff but I do have good days and bad days. Sometimes I have to do a draft three times. Writing is pleasurable but trying to get it published defeats many good authors. This is my fourteenth attempt and I shall give up this time because life is not a draft. I am sick and tired of rejection so I shall get this last attempt published myself if necessary. Publishers do not seem to realise what a lot of hard work goes into a book, even artichokes have hearts, but not publishers, it is a tough business! But I have every confidence that this second attempt at *Odes to Toads* is going to make it to the top.

The Strathmore docked at Tilbury and I was intrigued to see white labourers for the first time! The grey skies and the cold weather was beginning to depress me and I was not prepared to make England my home. Fortunately we were only on six months leave and I made the best of it because I knew that I would be returning to India on another three-year contract. Richard loved India and neither of us were prepared to settle down in the UK.

I was a little apprehensive about meeting my in-laws for the first time but I was in no hurry to go down to Bournemouth. I stayed with Mary and George when I arrived in England. They had a rented bungalow in Ash Vale and I was horrified to think that the loo was in the garden! It was a sweet little bungalow but I froze to death in the loo. I could not believe that I was living in Great Britain with such a primitive loo.

Ash Vale was in the heart of the country but I did not know how poor Mary survived out in the sticks! It is ironical that mental illness hit both Mary and Norine in England and I have also been under psychiatric care until recently. We are six in our family. My only brother and two other sisters take blood pressure tablets and I consider myself lucky to have joined them now. I think mental illness attacks sensitive people when they are plunged into a foreign environment. Our social life in Calcutta was very good. But when four of us married Englishmen and made our homes in England my two eldest sisters suffered breakdowns. They could not survive in England without servants. I never had this trouble because I love housework but both Mary and Norine were very fragile! When I met Mary again I could clearly see what the trouble was. One cannot transplant orchids and expect them to survive in an English garden! I class myself as a weed because I can survive anywhere as long as I am warm. It is the climate which kills off tropical flowers. Fortunately I married into a cultured middle-class family but both Mary and Norine did not. I warned Mary about George because he once worked in the same office as me. He was an uncultured cockney who had a good brain but no breeding.

I feel that it is not too late to save my sisters because I shall help them financially if my book hits the jackpot. I will give them all some money, including my brother. I have the best standard of living in the family and I want to see all of us continue to celebrate life to the fullest. We only live once, not twice, because not everyone gets a second chance so I intend to live it up from now on doing exactly what I want to do.

Richard drove Tessa and I to see his parents in Bournemouth one day and unfortunately we had arrived late for lunch. An elderly well-dressed lady strutted out towards the car when Richard rang the door bell. I was in the passenger seat with Tessa on my lap. How times have changed, this would be an offence nowadays.

Richard's mother ignored me totally and I heard her say,

'You're late as usual Richard. Violet does not like to be kept waiting,' she said rather sternly. Meanwhile I got out of the car and I walked towards the front door with Tessa in my arms. I soon got a glimpse of my aristocratic father-in-law who was standing in the hall. He was delighted to meet me and I noticed that he could not take his eyes off Tessa who had on a blue woollen crocheted ankle length dress looking just like a Victorian child. Her pale blue eyes matched her dress and I could see from the minute my beloved father-in-law set eyes on her he adored her. Tessa was the first granddaughter in the family and I believe she resembled my father-in-law's sister Mabel who died when she was quite young. I later heard that my father-in-law never got over Mabel's death and he kept on repeating 'Tessa is just like my sister Mabel,' he muttered over and over again and Tessa soon became aware of her importance. Richard's eldest brother John was also invited to lunch in order to break the ice. He was very handsome and he also had the marvellous Rumsey eyes!

My mother-in-law allowed us to have a quick drink in the drawing room and then we were all ushered into the dining room.

Violet had cooked the lunch but Mrs Parker did the waiting. My mother-in-law was a very elegant old lady and she was thoroughly spoilt by her husband. She also had striking blue eyes and glorious white hair. She was a tiny lady but my father-in-law was tall. His eyes were hazel like mine and I knew that he liked me as much as I liked him. Tessa sat in a high chair at the table and she soon dominated the conversation with her 'baby talk' and spoon banging. I was thoroughly embarrassed. My thoughts were far away during this family gathering but they soon returned when I heard that the conversation revolved round Richard's ex-fiancée. 'I don't know what you saw in her,' my father-in-law told Richard. I desperately wanted to stop the unpleasant conversation but Tessa did it for me instead.

She stood up in her high chair and spent an unending penny on my mother-in-law's brand new dining-room carpet. I quickly whisked her away into the bathroom and scolded her. 'How can you do such a naughty thing?' I asked her when I was removing her blue silk panties. But she looked at me defiantly and I read her thoughts 'They were talking nasty things about my daddy. I had to stop them,' she tried to tell me. It is ironical that right through my life Tessa has dealt with unpleasant situations. Later, many years later, Tessa would deal with a family crisis and I am eternally grateful to her. She has a will of iron and I could never be able to compete with her as a woman. Tessa is a very special lady and like all 'love children' God gives them a wonderful aura. These children have fought to come into this world and they all seem to make a great success of their lives. Abortion is a criminal act, it is murder of an unborn child which must be abolished. Animals never deliberately abort their young so why should humans commit this wicked act?

We returned to the dining room and I apologised for Tessa's bad behaviour. The carpet had been mopped up and John was helping to distract the attention Tessa created.

I liked John, he was the eldest son and he was not as prim and proper as Phillip who was the youngest. Richard was the middle son, he was undoubtedly the rebel in the family. I likened John and Phillip to two sentries who stood on either side of a carefully guarded domain – 'Rumsey and Rumsey' which was the estate agent family business. John was a qualified surveyor so he got in easily but Phillip who failed all the exams also got in because of his charm. He was undoubtedly my father-in-law's favourite son, so I had to guard my 'ps and qs'. Fortunately I get on equally well with men and women so my mother-in-law was not a great threat to me. I have the same attitude to both my sons' wives and to my son-in-law. I hate family quarrels, they are so unnecessary.

After lunch my father-in-law invited us to his office in order for me to see the flourishing family business and once again Tessa had to embarrass me. A secretary brought in a tray of tea and quite obviously the colour of the aluminium tray which was bright red caught Tessa's eye so she wanted to sit in it. I could not believe my eyes – she had the audacity to sit in the tray and spend another penny, much to my horror! I glanced at my father-in-law's face which showed me quite clearly that the tray would be thrown away and never used again. 'I'm sorry, Grandy, I think that Tessa is having trouble with her waterworks because of the cold. She has been potty trained from eleven months old. Perhaps silk panties are not a good idea for an eighteen month old child.' I started a perfectly normal conversation with my beloved father-in-law because I am a very natural person. He smiled but I think that the tray was definitely banished. We came back to the house and we moved into a delightful maisonette for the next six months, next door to my in-laws' house. Previously it was the staffs' quarters and Phillip and Mickie and their baby son occupied the flat above. John and Joyce had their own house with au pairs etc. but Phillip and Mickie were still tied to my mother-in-law's apron strings!

Richard refused to be tied to his parents and when he left Bryanston he moved up to London and he became an errand boy rather than obey his father. My father-in-law wanted Richard to be an architect but he refused to study for the exams because he was not good at maths. I admire Richard's guts to leave his wealthy family and branch out on his own. He joined the Territorial Army in London so when war was declared he was one of the first of many men who were called up. He boarded a ship bound for India but it was torpedoed so he had to return home. Nevertheless he boarded a second ship because we were destined to meet. Richard was in India doing various jobs for the army and navy. He even did courier work. Education is the finest thing a parent can give a child and because Richard was well educated he could do most jobs with skill.

He learnt to speak Hindi fluently from a Munshi, or teacher, so he was able to communicate with everyone. When I think back on Richard's life I have to admire his character. He was in India during the war and so was I but we never met one another. He told me that he helped to train my ex-fiancé in the gunnery school for navel officers in Bombay where he was known as 'boy'. I do not believe this story but anything was possible with Richard. He got engaged to a Wren lady doctor but his parents ruined their relationship. I believe his ex-fiancée had arranged to meet my in-laws in Bournemouth but they forgot all about it. His fiancée did have the guts to turn up at the house and she gave them a piece of her mind. 'Now I know why your son is like he is, it is because of you lot!' she said and she stormed out of the house back to Edinburgh. I had no idea that Richard was a very difficult person when I met him. My father-in-law described him beautifully as a baby. 'He had the face of an angel with lovely golden curls but the temper of a devil!' he told me. I believe John and Phillip shared a nanny but Richard had to have one to himself! Ironically Tessa had a temper in the morning when she was a little girl and the servants were very afraid of her. They all called her 'Muni Mah' even though she was only a child. I believe Mary Ayah had a lot of trouble with her in the morning as she would throw shoes at her.

Tessa had a vast wardrobe of dresses, play-suits and too many shoes which caused all the trouble in the morning.

My life in India was vastly different from my life in England. I had a retinue of servants when I married Richard. I had a cook, a bearer, a metha, and two nannies – Mary Ayah in the day and Mrs Gonez in the night.

The dhobi called once a week. I think I have mentioned this all before but I want to repeat it again because it is important.

I soon began to realise that life in the maisonette was hard. I did the cooking and cleaning myself and fortunately I had an excellent babysitter who did the ironing. She was a jewel because I hate ironing. I even had the courage to invite my in-laws over for dinner one night. I must recall a very amusing incident which happened that day. Richard and I were having a bath together and my poor mother-in-law was getting drenched outside from the overflow pipe. In a way it taught her not be such a busybody. I can laugh at this incident now but at the time I was very embarrassed. I think that Richard deliberately jumped into my bath in order to make this happen but I still remember being told off about it. Sometimes Granny, as I called her, was worse than Sister Ernestine, but I liked her in spite of the fact that she was a spitfire.

Richard and I went to Paris for a weekend in order to pick up our baby Renault which we were taking back to India. I loved Paris and the French clothes. We were only allowed to take out £40 in those days and I was able to purchase next summer's collection. I told the assistant that I was returning to India so she thought that it would be a good idea for me to buy the summer collection. Some of the outfits were semi-finished but I knew that my 'dersie' would soon put them together.

I think I got six lovely outfits for £40 something which would be unheard of now! I bought many French dresses from 'Madam

Andre' in Calcutta because they are chic and they seem to suit me.

We had a splendid night out at 'The Nouvelle Eve' which was a very up-market night club in Paris. It was the first time I saw a semi-nude show. I thought that the floor show was magnificent and I was not at all shocked because the French have a very elegant way of presenting these shows but unfortunately the English tend to be vulgar. I came to realise that Frenchmen are big flirts on the dance floor. Richard and I tend to do this as well so it was no surprise to us.

However, I never expected to be molested by a beautiful blonde girl who looked very much like Brigitte Bardot on the street. Richard and I were going to have a drink at a bar and we had no idea that we were walking past a lesbian dancehall. At first I thought that this pretty girl was after Richard but when she pushed him away and grabbed me I became alarmed. Fortunately Richard grabbed me back and we quickly crossed over to the bar which was on the opposite pavement. The barman gave us the news that the girl was searching for a dancing partner. I began to laugh hysterically but the tears rolled down my face as well. I have never forgotten this experience. If it happened today I would have ignored it. I like the French because the men and women have a charm of their own.

I had another amusing incident with the bidet in Paris. Richard was shaving at the basin when I came into the bathroom to have a shower or a bath. 'How can I wash my face in this contraption?' I asked Richard pointing to the bidet. 'I have never seen such a low wash basin,' I said staring at it in amazement.

Richard roared with laughter. 'It is a bidet, you have to sit on it and wash the lower part of your body,' he explained.

'But I want a bath or a shower,' I said giggling at my stupidity.

'This is France and we have not got a bathroom adjoining our room,' he told me.

I am glad to say that I think bidets are very hygienic and I would not be without one but I still prefer a shower to a bath!

We were delighted to get home to Bournemouth in our new baby Renault and to see Tessa again. Violet had looked after her on this lovely weekend. This six-month holiday in England was almost over so Richard and I took Tessa back with us to Mary's bungalow in Ash Vale because Richard wanted me to see the lake district. We had another enjoyable weekend as Mary and George looked after Tessa for us. I remember staying in a lovely hotel near Lake Windermere which was beautiful.

The scenery was out of this world. Richard also took me dancing one night to the Bagatelle in London. I loved dancing to Edmund de Ross's band and on the whole the holiday was a huge success but I could not wait to board the Jalhazard and return to India. As I stood on the deck waving goodbye to Mary and George I broke down and cried. I did not want to leave Mary alone in this dreary island called England. When I arrived the people looked drab, they mainly dressed in different shades of brown, but what a contrast we have today! I love England which is now my home because it is full of colourful people. The immigrants have enhanced the country and one day I hope we will have a world without any boundaries and people can be free to live anywhere. As I saw this tiny island disappear into the heavy mist I could not wait to arrive at Bombay where I met Olive again. We did the long train journey from Bombay to Calcutta by train and when we arrived at Howrah Station I was delighted to see Norine and my servants, especially Mary Ayah who had come to greet us. The bustling station took on the old familiar sound 'Parn, beerie, cigarette' which the vendors shouted out aloud throughout India.

Ode to married life in India

I was back on familiar ground again and for the next three years Richard rented an apartment opposite St Paul's Cathedral in Chowringhee. It was a charming place with lovely marble floors. Richard turned it into a little palace. We worked very well together, Richard did all the carpentry making pelmets, a dressing table for me, and a very functional ironing board for Mary Ayah which I wish I had now. He bought teak furniture, sanded it down and then rubbed in a kind of chalk which had a marvellous effect. I miss my talented husband and if I had my life over again I would have still married Richard. We were excellent 'workmates', not 'soulmates'. I was to find a soulmate many years later when I entered the pink period of my life.

For the next three years I enjoyed a life of luxury. We were woken each morning when the bearer brought 'pulling ka char', or morning tea, in bed at about 7 a.m. A cooked breakfast was had around 9 a.m. Lunch was served at one o'clock, tea was taken in the drawing room at about 4 p.m. and dinner normally began at 9 p.m. Gin and tonics were served before lunch and whisky was drunk after sundown.

Tessa was taken for two walks a day in the grounds of St Paul's Cathedral or the maiden. All the ayahs would sit around and chat whilst their charges played with one another. Some of them knitted and others did embroidery. Mary Ayah was a good needlewoman. She had been my sister Mary's ayah in Bangalore and she worked as a lady's maid. Looking after children was new to Mary Ayah but I soon taught her the ropes. She was unmarried but she lived with a cook.

Living together was normal amongst our servants especially if one had a Christian ayah who had a non Christian boyfriend. I like to think that Mary Ayah was living with her uncle who was a cook, she told me this story and I believe her.

I was lucky to get her from my sister Mary who brought her to me from Bangalore. Mary was on her way to England and poor Richard had to accommodate Mary Ayah for a while because I was living in the YWCA. Indian servants like to work for the same family and it was quite common to hand down servants to one another. I loved the servants because they were very dedicated people, often leaving their own families in the country for months in order to work in the large towns and cities.

I believe that India has changed a lot now and nobody has servants anymore. I cannot believe this because I am sure if I returned I would soon find a servant. I hope the railways have not changed as India had marvellous trains.

I still remember some of the names EIR, GIP, BB & CI and in addition to the famous vendors who shouted 'Parn, beerie, cigarettes' little men carried goblets of 'Parni' (water), shouting their heads off. One can be born or die on an Indian railway station and nobody would bat an eyelid. It was home to a multitude of beggars and a free hospital for the dying! Terribly tragic when one thinks about it deeply. I would like to take Tessa and Simon to India one day and show them the land of my birth. A couple of years ago my granddaughter Sophie stayed in the same YWCA in Calcutta as I did. She even took the trouble to have my beloved mother's grave restored which was very kind of her. Kate will be going to India next year. Tessa's mother-in-law and I were both born in India. All the best people were!

We never went on 'home leave' again but we did take Tessa once to Gopalpur when she was a baby. The sea was as rough as the breakers in Hawaii and I nearly drowned. This nasty episode has made me dislike the sea because I still remember this awful accident.

I was holding Mary Ayah's hand and she was holding the fisherman's hand but she accidentally let his hand go and I got swept away by huge breakers. My thoughts were with Tessa. 'Who is going to feed her?' I thought because I was still nursing her. My fears were unnecessary because the fishermen were excellent swimmers and I was soon rescued as breaker after breaker tried to swallow me up. Fortunately I held my breath until I was grabbed and pulled out to safety. I have always hated the sea and that is why I never learnt to swim. When we were young working girls we had a couple of holidays in Gopalpur which also attracted many lonely servicemen during the war. I remember a couple of them asking me if they could rub me down with sun cream and I allowed them to do so. They were so gentle; all they wanted was to feel a woman's skin and I saw no harm in it whatsoever.

Men have always treated me with great respect and none of them dared to overstep the mark. I did meet a few toads as well but I prefer to remember the many men who loved me. Now I want to give some love back to all the lonely people by writing my musical autobiography in order to cheer everyone up. The wartime music is remembered by many people. I believe Her Majesty the Queen and Prince Phillip fell in love to 'People Will Say We're in Love' and so did Richard and I at the Golden Slipper Night Club. Richard had a bout of dysentery when I first met him which was very common in India so he was in The Elgin Nursing Home for treatment. I went to see him regularly with a friend of his and this is when I began to realise he needed someone to look after him. He looked so fragile in bed in his striped pyjamas but he was certainly not bored because he was doing a marvellous cartoon of a surgeon doing an operation. Several organs had been removed including the heart and they were hanging on a line in the theatre. He wrote a witty remark which read 'Obviously nothing wrong with him – let's start re-assembling.' I shall be putting some meaningful cartoons at the end of the book so that people will also remember Richard. He was a brilliant designer and he designed the second largest cigarette hoarding in the world in Calcutta, enticing people to smoke; a bad habit which he had for many years. He did manage to kick the habit in the end but it was too late.

British firms were targeted when the Indians got their independence. We knew that this would be Richard's last contract in India so we made the most of it. The social life in India was rather limited amongst a few friends, but I enjoyed the home life with my retinue of servants. I was never lonely like in England because there was always a servant at hand to talk to. I saw Tessa briefly during the day she was usually playing with friends in the maiden but last thing at night she used to be brought by Mary

Ayah to say 'goodnight'. She used a delightful phrase 'Tessa's going "chuckaby".' She used to clasp her head in her little hands and pretend to be asleep. Tessa was the best dressed little girl because Mary Ayah made sure of that!

She did her hair in charming hair styles every day. I would never like to lead the shallow life I had in India again. We had The Saturday Club and The Swimming Club where we met friends. The various hotels like The Great Eastern, The Grand, Firpos etc. were popular on weekends because they had live bands and a floor show. The food was excellent value and both Richard and I enjoyed the dancing. We had two cinemas, the 'Metro' and the 'Lighthouse' – I have no idea what life is like there now. I have heard that it has changed for the worse.

Four years later, almost to the exact date, I had another caesarean and Simon was born. I could have had him on Tessa's birthday which is on 4 April but I foolishly asked Tessa 'Do you want a new baby for your birthday or do you want a party?'

'I want my party,' she replied and consequently Simon was born on 6 April. I could not believe that Simon was a boy until I had a secret peep! I employed Lucy Ayah for Simon. Ayahs came and went as they did with all the 'memsahibs', or ladies but Mary Ayah was always happy to return when needed. Mrs Gomez was no longer required. The weeks flew past with a new baby in the house and before I knew it Richard and I were on our way back to the UK. The servants garlanded us up to our chins with beautiful flowers and just before the train moved out of Howrah Station Mary Ayah handed Tessa over to Richard and Lucy Ayah put Simon in my arms. As usual we did the long journey by train from Calcutta to Bombay because I was not prepared to fly. I made sure I had a good supply of soft muslin nappies which I threw away en route. In a way I had invented the first 'disposable nappy', but when I came back to England I used lovely Harrington nappies which I kept snow-white with 'Fairy Snow'. My neighbours in Walton-on-Thames always admired Simon's whiter than white nappies! I had a secret – I always believed in soaking my nappies overnight in buckets, one bucket was for the soiled nappies and the other one was for the wet ones.

My first home in England was not my mother-in-law's

maisonette which she had lent us when we were on leave. I had a cold bleak room across the road. Mrs Hughes was a very kind lady, she rented one small bedroom to the three of us – Tessa, Simon and I – and Richard joined us on weekends. Richard lived in the RNVR Club in London until he found a job in advertising. Unfortunately Mrs Hughes' daughter had whooping cough, but I never knew about it until Simon who was only three months old got it. This lonely period of my life made me into a full-time mother. I brought out my Singer sewing machine and I made Simon a warm cosy sleeping blanket. I designed and made it myself so that I did not need to worry about him being cold because I zipped him into it at night. I also bought new satin bindings for all my blankets and machined them on which made them look brand new! Mrs Hughes gave us breakfast and a high tea and my mother-in-law gave us lunch. This was one of the loneliest periods of my life even though I had my in-laws living directly opposite me and my brother-in-law Phillip and his wife living in the flat above. I did get *one* invitation to tea from my sister-in-law in the six months.

Violet was a good cook so we enjoyed a nice lunch every day but when tripe and onions turned up Tessa would roll it about in her mouth. 'For God's sake Mary, give the child something else,' my beloved father-in-law would say. I always thought of 'Scrooge' whenever tripe and onions was served which fortunately was not too often.

My in-laws had a very nice Victorian House which was full of antiques but it was in Boscombe. I liked Boscombe much better than Bournemouth as I was able to cut through Boscombe Gardens to the beach when my sister-in-law Mickie allowed us to use her beach hut. It was a very sad period of my life because Richard had no job and I had no home. I used to take the children for walks and the orange boards advertising Rumsey and Rumsey properties for sale stood out like grave stones!

My in-laws were dealers of property but they had no idea what was going through my mind. In my opinion the family were rich but none of them, except for my father-in-law, knew how to give.

I got into serious trouble one day when I left Violet in charge of Simon when Tessa and I went shopping to buy my in-laws a little cake for their wedding anniversary. In my haste to get back in time for lunch I fell as I was getting off the bus and I laddered my stockings. When I got back my mother-in-law was furious.

'In England we never leave a baby with a soiled nappy,' she rebuked me and I replied with equally harsh words.

'In India we have nurseries for our children and we do not have them in a kitchen with the smell of cabbage about!' She walked out in a temper in a smart suit, hand-made shoes, and a hat to go to bridge. I was allowed to use the dining room after lunch and my father-in-law normally attended to his stamp collection in the drawing room. I believe once he had to put my cantankerous mother-in-law up on the wardrobe to teach her a lesson. Perhaps he should have left her there! After this nasty episode I wrote her a sharp note 'Why is it that you who has so much should be jealous of me who has so little?' Richard had sent me some flowers which made her very angry. 'Richard knows I love flowers! why reproach me for this little gift?' I asked. I returned the £1.00 which was my birthday present with my note. But later that evening my in-laws enjoyed their wedding anniversary cake. I found it difficult to eat because with every mouthful I thought of how cruel my mother-in-law had been to me. My romantic character made me buy that cake which got me into serious trouble. It may be because I have been an orphan from the age of sixteen I was determined to have a good home of my own one day. It may be for this same reason I now share my delightful home with lodgers!

God has sent Robyn, my South African lodger into my home when I needed her most.

Robyn flew into my nest a few weeks ago and she has given me a purpose for living. She is a bright, caring, young lady and I cannot understand how Fi and Robyn are still unmarried. Career girls have a special aura about them and I think that men are threatened by their intelligence. Marriage seems to be for deadly dull people! Most men want a 'glorified housekeeper' which is the worst job in the world. All husbands should pay their wives at least £15,000 a year with board and lodging thrown in. This is definitely a man's world but it is good to see that it is changing and I feel that very soon women will be able to call the tune! I hope I will live long enough to see that day.

Ode to a Basement Flat in Hampstead

It took Richard six months to find a suitable job which also meant he had found a flat for me in Hampstead. I have always been very psychic and as soon as I approached the front door I knew that something dreadful had happened in this flat but I went in calmly and I tried to make it into a home. The first job that caught my eye was the filthy gas stove. I took it all to bits and I cleaned it thoroughly but when it came to re-assembling all the burners etc. I was unable to do it and I burst out crying. I eventually dried my tears and I went to the lady who lived opposite me and I approached her housekeeper for help. This kind lady was only too happy to oblige. I shall never forget that basement flat in Hampstead. I often looked at the people walking on the pavement from my bedroom window because I did not believe that I was actually living underground. However, it did have a back garden which was very run down. The curtains were dingy but I cleverly hung my own curtains from India in front of them and the whole atmosphere changed. I scattered colourful cushions and I soon transformed what was a derelict home into a comfortable one.

The landlady actually complimented me on my taste and she was soon able to rent the flat again because she asked me not to remove my furnishings until she got another tenant.

I liked my neighbours who were all anxious to meet me. I was asked by many inquisitive people whether I liked the flat and my reply was, 'Something awful has happened here,' I told them. One day my cleaner Anne told me the tragic story. The flat was owned by a charming South African man who was having a lot of trouble with his wife and one day after a terrible argument she left him with her two children. The poor man was devastated so he gassed himself. 'I knew it Anne,' I told my cleaner, 'because I am psychic!'

I was not afraid of this friendly ghost because he had left all his beautiful silver hairs on my bed to keep me warm! I could not bear the cold weather in England and this is when I got my first attack of cystitis which is a very painful complaint. I have had this nasty complaint for many years and each attack gets worse. I was very ill over the weekend but my GP has put me on medication from today. I hope to bounce back and forget this nasty ailment which attacks many women. Old age does not come alone it brings many trials and troubles with it!

Phillip accompanied us to Hampstead. I suspect my father-in-law sent him to see our new home. I remember it was a bitterly cold day and Phillip had to shovel the snow from the front door. He went back to Bournemouth shortly after we arrived after seeing the apartment. I gave Richard bacon and eggs for dinner, it was the first meal I had cooked in my life. Richard enjoyed his meal and complimented me on my cooking. 'Anyone who can cook bacon and eggs well can cook!' I agree with that because I hate greasy bacon and eggs.

A fried egg should be lightly cooked in the bacon fat and if I have to fry an egg alone I pour a little olive oil in the pan and I cook it gently, unlike an omelette which is done quickly.

I enjoyed living in Hampstead and when I heard that a local launderette had opened I was the first customer.

I wheeled poor little Simon in his pram with a huge bag of washing almost on top of him! Tessa walked sweetly by my side holding on to the pram. Tessa and Simon were very obedient children. They were brought up with strict discipline until the age of seven and neither of them have given me a day's trouble. Unlike my grandchildren who give Tessa a lot of hassle.

We enjoyed our walks to Primrose Hill. I took the children out twice a day because I wanted to continue the same routine as India. I did very well but I was anxious to move out of London and have a house of our own preferably near London. Richard saw one advertised in Walton-on-Thames which he liked and we saw it at night, because we had a baby-sitter.

Ode to Cherwell

I actually saw 'Cherwell' at midnight! It was a lovely moonlit night but my heart sank! Richard was full of enthusiasm but I could see by moonlight that it was going to be very hard work. We only paid £3,250 for 'Cherwell' but I was soon to realise that the old Edwardian house had three major faults – damp, dry rot and wood worm! John surveyed the house and he told Richard that he would have trouble re-selling it.

My in-laws came up from Bournemouth to see the house and my beloved father-in-law paid for all the beautiful mahogany furniture because 'Cherwell' did not have any fitted wardrobes. I loved my mahogany wardrobes, they were beautifully made and I spent the next eight years lovingly polishing my furniture until they sparkled! My mother-in-law made a cutting remark before they drove back to Bournemouth. 'We'll see you in eight years!' she said.

She was absolutely right because it took Richard and I exactly eight years to transform 'Cherwell' which was a derelict ruin into a lovely family home.

I still remember the estate agents description of it when we came to sell it. 'Gracious living! Charming family home consisting of a spacious hall, a drawing room, dining room, breakfast room, kitchen and a downstairs cloakroom. Plus four bedrooms, bathroom and separate toilet. The property is in immaculate order.' And I should have added, 'one worn out lady!' I worked from morning till night on this house because I had and still do have very high standards! I eventually got a cleaner once a week and she and I became very good friends. Christine, who helped me to clean the house, and I both met up with each other years later under very unfortunate circumstances. Life is funny because Christine and I were wonderful workers and we landed up in a mental hospital! I wonder why? Tessa is right 'Life's a bitch and then you die.'

But now is not the time to think of depression because when I was living in 'Cherwell' I was a vivacious young mother with a wonderful handy husband and two lovely children. Richard was 'Jack of all Trades' and I was his labourer. I learnt how to mix concrete and I carried the heavy buckets up the stairs and handed them to Richard who was on a ladder outside tiling the windowsills. I had boundless energy and no job was too big or hard for me.

I also helped to make a drive, bashing the hardcore with a sledge hammer much to Simon's delight, he was watching me from his pram. He thought that it was a lot of fun but I knew that it was jolly hard work. Richard could only help me on Sundays because at one time husbands had to go to work on Saturday morning. I bashed on with the hardcore and many workmen on their bicycles waved out to me and said 'Now you know what hard work is!' I use to wave back and laugh! 'Cherwell' was a very happy house! I did most impossible things.

If I needed a gardener I asked the postman and very soon he became my gardener. If I needed a dilapidated porch pulled down I asked my plumber and he brought his brother on a Sunday and they pulled my porch down for me.

Tradesmen turned up and I had a way of getting them to help me. One day I met my plumber in a most unusual way. Christine, my home help, was cleaning my breakfast room and when she saw water pouring from the ceiling she drew my attention to the fact that I had a burst pipe! Something unheard of in India. Simon enjoyed this calamity because he loved wading in the water but I was horrified! Christine's husband was an electrician and the word soon spread and everyone would turn up for work.

I have always been a very active person and it is too late to change my personality now. I would rather die like my father did of a massive stroke than sit in a chair in an old people's home. I have had five consultants interested in my case and I should be in the *Guinness Book of Records* classified as 'a survivor'.

Why am I a survivor? It is because I believe that everything will work out well in the end with God's help. I have a very optimistic character and fortunately I see most people through rose-tinted glasses. I do believe that all my doctors have done their best for me and now it is time for me to pay them back. This book would not have been 'born' if the ringing noise in my head was knocked out by a psychiatrist. Books, like babies, must *not* be aborted. I am glad that my consultant endocrinologist has given me another chance to be heard. I have grabbed this chance and I am doing my best to prove that I am a writer! God gives everyone a 'talent' and it is a good idea to use it before we die and leave this great big beautiful world some happiness for future generations to enjoy.

Everyone likes music and dancing. Perhaps I should call my musical autobiography 'Let's Dance!' How can I be depressed again when I see what I have achieved? Many elderly people still enjoy music and dancing and we can invite the young to enjoy it as well. The year 2002 will be the beginning of 'The Romantic Revolution'. We need words to be able to communicate with one another and the only way I can communicate with my readers is to write. I am certain that many women will be able to identify with me because most women are romantic creatures but poor men are 'functional machines'. A relationship breaks down when couples do not talk. For instance if a husband wants good sex at night he should begin to woo his wife at breakfast. A hug, a kiss and most importantly tell her that you love her. These three little words 'I love you' mean a lot to a woman!

It was in 'Cherwell' that I got seriously ill. The hard work had caught up with me. I frequently visited my GP complaining about tiredness and heavy periods. He eventually sent me to a consultant gynaecologist who prescribed some pills for me which gave me a head full of cysts but it did nothing to stop the heavy bleeding. We sisters were having a family reunion at 'Cherwell' that year.

Olive arrived from Bombay and Lynnette and her two children Brian and Kathy flew in from Canada. I stopped my medication because it had bad side effects and I concentrated on this lovely family reunion instead. We toured the country and called on Mary, Norine and Claude so it was great fun. We are a very united family and Olive and Lynette had made this family reunion possible. We sang together again and 'Cherwell' became an even happier home. Tessa and Simon came to know their

Canadian cousins and I look back on this period of my life with great happiness. Lynette's husband was Cornish but I refer to the children as being Canadian because they had picked up the accent! Unfortunately this delightful holiday came to an end far too quickly and I cried bitterly on their departure. My sisters noticed that I had changed. 'Why are you so quiet "B"?' they would ask me.

'Nobody talks to one another in England. We greet each other and then we talk about the weather. I no longer stop and chat to people unless I know them well. Since arriving in England I feel very lonely. All I do is housework day and night. I have grown to love it. My home and my children are my best friends. I only see Richard late at night, we seem to be drifting apart,' I told them confidentially. The girls were very upset to see the change in my personality but it was due to the fact that I was very ill.

After Olive and Lynette returned home I went to see my GP again and this time he actually examined me and he looked alarmed. 'Are you sure you're not pregnant because if you are not you must have an urgent operation. Give me your husband's telephone number,' he said anxiously. He discussed the urgent operation which he thought should be done 'privately' in order to get it done quickly. My beloved father-in-law assured Richard that he would pay the bill so I went immediately into The Princess Christian Nursing Home in Windsor. I met the young surgeon who was going to do the operation and my GP told me that he was also going to assist.

Later I heard this GP was a failed surgeon but he was still interested in surgery. In my eyes he was a failed GP and because of his neglect I grew a tumour the size of a full term foetus. I think he covered up this fault by getting a friend to perform the urgent operation in Windsor. This is when I began to distrust GPs who do not have enough time to help their patients!

As soon as I arrived at the nursing home I settled down for the night. The next morning I had a lovely hot bath and perfumed myself with 'Ma Griffe' which had a tenacious smell! I did not like the injection I was given which made my heart race but I calmed down when I realised that my surgeon was also in my room and he told me not to panic. 'It will soon be over,' he assured me. I believe the theatre smelt of 'Ma Griffe' and the medical staff made a joke of it.

'Which theatre does she think she is going to?' they asked one another but my GP said 'It's just like her, she is a very feminine lady!' However when the surgeon cut my abdomen open the anaesthetist and the theatre sister threatened to down tools because they were both Catholics. I believe my surgeon had a second look at the X-rays and he was convinced that the tumour had no bones so he decided to proceed with the operation. It was a very serious one and I was told all the gory details when I became stronger. I spent one month in the nursing home until my surgeon discharged me.

Ironically when my period was due I began to get hot flushes and severe palpitations. Nature was rebelling against what the surgeon had done to me. These hot sweats and palpitations frightened me but I was determined to leave the nursing home and go home. 'I want to get well for the summer,' I told my surgeon. My foreign children need me,' I explained.

'Why do you take foreign students?' he asked. He obviously had a one track mind!

'I need the money, besides I do not want my children to suffer from xenophobia,' I told him.

'Do you take boys or girls?' he asked suspiciously.

'I take both. I belong to an agency and I take what they give me,' I said to which he replied most emphatically: 'No boys this year!' Then he cracked a joke. 'A woman like you will feel twenty years younger,' he added.

'Well then I shall feel seventeen!' I replied. I am now seventy-eight years old but I still feel seventeen! The body alters but not the brain. When Richard arrived to take me home the surgeon told him 'Take her away to the country where the air is bracing,' he suggested. And before I knew it I found that I was on my way to Cornwall! Richard had arranged it all. Our little mini had cushions and blankets scattered all over the car to keep me comfortable for the long journey and I was thrilled to see Tessa and Simon tucked in the back seat. The long journey was tiring and I felt every little bump. My body felt hollow and I was unable to walk without assistance because I was so weak.

I was glad when the journey was over. I went straight to bed and that evening I experienced hot flushes and palpitations again. I compared myself to a tiny sailing boat which was having my colourful sails torn to shreds. I held Richard's hand for comfort. Fortunately these hot flushes soon passed and then I imagined I was sailing on to calmer waters! If I did not use my vivid imagination I would not have been able to handle this ghastly experience. Richard also spent the weekend with us in Mount Pleasant. Eric and Pat, his wife, had a dairy farm in Poughill where we spent many happy summers so we were going to spend the next three months with them. Tessa and Simon enjoyed the local school and we had a very happy time. I would see their little heads bobbing up and down as they meandered through the Cornish lanes which have very tall hedges. I was having problems with my waterworks again but I ignored it because I was happy. I bought some wool and I began knitting and Tessa who was only eleven also knitted a lovely warm pullover for Simon. Richard came down from Walton-on-Thames every weekend to visit us.

I did not know how he coped with the tedious journey but Richard has always loved driving vast distances. The bracing air and the good farm cooking did make me much stronger but the aches and pains in all my joints accompanied by fluid retention became a problem.

The children always accompanied me on my walks down the long drive, they walked one on either side of me until one day I got the courage to walk down to the post box on my own to post Richard a letter. The cows happened to be returning for milking and as I was still very weak I broke down and cried because they blocked my path. Eric, the farmer, was amused to see me in the middle of the herd in tears. 'They are only cows, not wild animals Bridget,' he told me.

Our lovely three months holiday came to an end but I had the summer to look forward to.

I did as my surgeon said – I took no boys that summer. Marie-Pierre brought a friend called Fabienne with her, they were both doctors' daughters. I had had Marie-Pierre for two previous summers. She lived in Paris and so did Fabienne and I was glad to see them. All my foreign children treated me like a mother and some of them never wanted to go home again. Simon was greatly loved by the girls who used to spoil him and one year he sobbed his heart out when Marie-Claude a twenty-one year old French girl returned home. Marie-Claude spent the winter with us that year and she was a great companion to all of us. She eventually married her boyfriend but I believe that she, like many of my foreign children, divorced. It is sad that Simon whom I thought would be the last person to divorce has done likewise. I also caught up with Marie-Pierre one day in Guildford when I was shopping. 'Mrs Rumsey! Mrs Rumsey!' I heard the young woman call waving her hands up in the air. 'What are you doing here, Marie-Pierre?' I asked.

I invited her home to 'Noirmont Place' and I heard the full story. Marie-Pierre like me had to get married but she divorced her husband when her son was born. She may still be living in England. If nothing else is accomplished by writing this book it might help me to get in touch with all my foreign children who are scattered all over the world! I would dearly love to see all of them again. I have lost touch with most of them as, like Tessa and Simon, they must be too busy with their own lives.

Ode to Imagination

I entered the pink period of my life quite by chance when I brought Tessa and Simon back from school one day. I saw a piece of paper on the mat in the hall which read 'If you cannot go to Spain, let Spain come to you.' I picked it up excitedly and read it out aloud to the children. 'What an unusual way of asking someone to be a host to a Spanish student,' I thought, not realising this simple note was going to change my life forever.

I dialled the telephone number immediately and I asked to speak to the person concerned, who happened to be a Spanish priest called Father Ubago. I told him that I had a twelve-year-old daughter and a son of eight. I thought that it would be a good idea to have a student of the same age as Tessa so that she would be able to take him to parties and have fun with him and my request was accepted. I was introduced to Pablo who was a typical boy, he knew little or no English. All he wanted to do was to ride a bike round and round the garden. I moved heaven and earth for this strange little boy in order that Tessa could play tennis with him but all my attempts ended in failure.

'Mummy I hate Pablo, he is an animal,' Tessa said one day when she returned from a game of tennis with this horrid little boy. I had been brought up by Catholic nuns but I was determined that Tessa would meet boys from an early age.

Tessa and Simon were attending Danesfield School which was a co-educational private school because I was determined that my children would not grow up like me. I have an outgoing personality but I cannot have an intimate relationship with anybody. I am a 'romantic' and nobody can change my personality. During the pink period of my life I almost became human and I went through the highs and the lows normal people experience everyday.

Pablo was a disaster and as Father Ubago visited the host families frequently he became aware of it. 'I am going to send this boy back to Madrid,' he said one day.

'But Father I have never failed in my job, please let me persevere. Perhaps I can turn him into a gentleman,' I pleaded.

'No he has to go back today,' he said impatiently.

'But Father please—' I was not allowed to finish my sentence.

'Pablo,' he commanded, 'pack your things you are going back to Madrid,' he told him. I saw that there was no point arguing with Father Ubago so I rushed upstairs and I packed Pablo's suitcase. But before Father Ubago left he told me most sincerely 'I will bring you a boy, well he is really a young man, who will show Tessa that all Spanish boys are not like animals,' he assured me.

'He is living with a family in Wimbledon and he is very unhappy. He belongs to one of the most important families in Madrid. You will like him,' he said with a twinkle in his eye! Dear Father Ubago became like a magician casting a spell and my imagination ran wild. 'I shall bring him tomorrow but now I must go,' he added hastily. I was left at the door spellbound. As I waved goodbye to Father Ubago I began to wonder what this important boy was like. Daniel, another Spanish boy, told me that I would like him.

'Do you know him Daniel?' I asked inquisitively.

'No, he comes from a very closed family. He has his own circle of friends,' he replied. Daniel was living with a friend of mine and when he popped in he did tell me about Father Ubago's plans but I did not discuss it further.

As promised Father Ubago turned up the next day for tea. I drove in with the children and to my surprise he had arrived early. He was grinning from ear to ear on the door step.

'I'm sorry I'm late,' I told him.

'No, you are not late, Mrs Rumsey. I am early,' he replied.

This charming priest had captivated me but I noticed that he was alone. 'Where's the boy?' I asked all flustered.

'He's in the car, I shall bring him in in a minute,' he said. I quickly put the kettle on and brought in the trolley of goodies for tea. Father Ubago sat down and had his tea keeping the boy waiting in the car. Every move of his was theatrical as if he was playing a trump card. After his tea he made a final move 'I am going to get the boy' he announced. The drawing room was full of children and when he made his entrance again he was followed by a handsome young boy dressed in a smart suit. He did not look like a boy, he was a young executive! My thoughts were racing but when Father Ubago introduced us : 'Mrs Rumsey this is Cesar,' he said graciously I only heard the words 'Cleopatra this is your Cesar— have fun with him!' Cesar stepped forward and took my hand to kiss it but at the same time he gave me a wicked wink. I could not believe it. Everyone stared at us in astonishment but I had eyes only for Tessa as I saw her across the room. Tessa, I said in my thoughts, I am going to keep Cesar for you until you grow up. I was thirty-eight years old and Cesar was sixteen and Tessa was twelve.

'I began to remember my surgeon's words, 'A woman like you will feel twenty years younger which meant that I was eighteen and Cesar was two years younger! Darling Tessa was only twelve but from that tender age she knew what I was planning for her. Tessa and I were very close once we were more like sisters than mother and daughter. I had the same relationship with Simon and having close contact with both my young children for many years kept me young. I spoke to them as equals but they always respected me unlike my grandchildren who can be very argumentative with their parents.

After tea Father Ubago made a hasty departure and I did the washing up at the sink alone watching the children playing in the garden. Cesar took off his jacket and placed it on the apple tree, he had on a spotless white shirt and smart tie. But I felt that he should change into something more comfortable like jeans and a tea shirt. I interrupted the game of badminton and I told him to get changed which he did but the expression on his face was one of surprise. I read his thoughts. How dare you tell me to change my clothes? My mother would never have attempted to do this, I heard him saying.

Now whether my reader is going to believe me or not I have to explain that from the minute I met Cesar we spoke to one another without words. Our thoughts did all the talking! Words were not necessary. We spoke with our eyes, with our hands, with our smiles and above all with laughter. We laughed at the same things at the same time. The meeting place was in the breakfast room and sometimes we were as many as eight at the table but yet we were able to communicate above everyone else because we communicated silently. I remember driving him home after a party on a gorgeous moonlit night by the river in order for him to break his silence but all he did was to stare at me with his wicked Spanish eyes as if he was reading my thoughts. We never spoke a word and yet I remember that night as if it happened yesterday. All my children went out to parties and I was the taxi that took them to the parties and brought them home.

I also gave many parties for my foreign children's friends and Richard and I often joined the young ones in the conservatory. Richard and Eddie, my twenty-one-year-old Swiss boy, put up the extension in the summer together so that the children could have their own fun. Eddie's sister was an air hostess and she brought him to 'Cherwell'. He was a very nice boy and the first thing he did was to sit on a stool in the front garden and paint a picture of 'Cherwell'. I still have Eddie's painting hanging up in my downstairs cloakroom. Cesar sent me a copy of the Desiderata when he was in Harvard University.

Both these boys were artists so they understood my character very well. The Desiderata is also hanging in the same cloakroom as Eddie's painting. I must meet all my foreign children again one day and we can have a grand family reunion! In a way I have been introducing people from all parts of the world to the British way of life so perhaps the Queen may make me a Lady? My name is Brid-get and I have been trying for many years to bridge the gap between north, south, east and west of the world so that we can all accept black, white and yellow people as being part of the human race. I did this through young people because adults are too old to change. In order to have a better world we have to educate the children because children do not suffer from xenophobia. I love watching children play but I think that everyone is gradually growing together nowadays.

The summer of 1962 passed happily like all my summers, and it was not until it was over that I realised how lonely I was. It was on Cesar's last night when we were listening to 'Young at Heart' sung by Frank Sinatra, I felt Cesar's eyes stripping my soul. We were undoubtedly 'soulmates' I have been looking for this kind of relationship all my life and God had sent me one at last. In my opinion there are four different kinds of love – romantic love, courtly love, passionate love and unconditional love. The Oedipus complex is not love it is an illness. Richard and Tessa saw Cesar off next morning but I lay in bed late because I could not say goodbye, it was too final. Cesar knocked on my door and he said goodbye, but I could not reply.

When Richard drove out of the drive I rushed into Cesar's room to wave goodbye but I was too late. I looked at his bed and I slipped my hands down his sheets, they were still warm then I burst into tears. It was only yesterday during lunch I was asked to have a twenty-one-year-old French boy and I had accepted him. Cesar heard the telephone call himself so I quickly dried my eyes and got down to stripping Cesar's bed and preparing a fresh bed for Jacques.

I tried not to get emotional with my foreign children but I did with several of them because some children have a special place in my heart. I have a child-like personality myself, not childish, and I am inclined to trust people. When they turn on me I cannot accept it. I am easily hurt and that is why I only love people romantically because I think that romantic love is the best and I will remain a romantic forever!

Richard took us to Spain the following Spring and Cesar invited us to his parents' apartment in Madrid. It was a palatial apartment and walking into the dining room for lunch could be compared to walking into a stately home. The dining table was enormous and we were served by butlers and maids who wore long white gloves. I had no idea that Cesar's parents were so rich. Cesar's father was enchanted with Simon's table manners and he arranged for Ivan to accompany Cesar in the summer because Cesar's parents were very impressed with their eldest son's behaviour on his return from England. I had four sons pass through my hands, for the next eight years each one spent two summers with me, so we got to know this important banking family very well. Ironically I appeal to bankers because I am like a cheque which will never bounce! The American Air Force captain was a banker, Cesar is a banker and I looked after my retired bank manager for four and a half years. Bankers are excellent judges of character they have to be in order to survive in banking. I sold 'Cherwell' when we returned from Spain all due to my good bank manager who was a personal friend.

After lunch we relaxed in one of the intimate drawing rooms and Cesar's mother began to talk to me. I could not take my eyes off a life-size painting of a handsome young Army officer. Cesar's mother saw me gazing at him as if I knew him.

'He is Cesar's uncle,' she explained. 'His name is also Cesar,' she added smiling at my curiosity. 'All my women friends admire him.'

I smiled back at her but my thoughts were going around in circles. Perhaps Cesar's uncle made me ask Richard to take us to Madrid. I was convinced that Cesar's uncle was my soulmate. My Spanish grandmother Sophie died during childbirth when she was very young. Cesar probably had his uncle's soul and I had my Spanish grandmother's, this was the fatal attraction! Perhaps God allows young souls to return to earth in order to have a second chance of finding love! I preferred to keep my relationship with Cesar a romantic one because in my opinion romantic love is sacred and it lasts for ever. I had ruined my life when I had a physical affair with Richard so when I met Cesar I had been a romantic for years. I intend to be a romantic until I die. I found that Cesar's mother had a delightful personality and we got on very well together. She tried to explain that the whole of Madrid knew that her son had met me and I told her that the whole of Weybridge knew about Cesar! I have always been able to understand foreigners so we carried on talking in sign language etc. until it was time for us to proceed on our journey to Marbella. It was a very tiring journey which was done in a tiny mini but Richard and I were young and we were able to take the strain. We almost stopped at San Sebastian overnight but when I saw the room I refused to accept it. The maids were not surprised when I told them that the last occupant of this sinister room jumped on to the railway track and committed suicide. I have mentioned that I am very psychic and the maids told me that my vision was true! I am afraid I know when tragedy is going to strike but there is nothing I can do about it. We had dinner at the hotel and we drove through the night. Tessa and Simon were very tired but Richard showed no sign of fatigue. We spent a very pleasant holiday with Richard's advertising friends who had retired early to Spain.

Ode to Park Place

We moved to 'Park Place' in the spring so the following summer we were living in Weybridge.

'Park Place' was one of four detached houses tucked away from Woodland Grove. It was a small modern house built in the Georgian style. I did not realise that none of my beautiful furniture would fit into this house until the removal van arrived. Furniture was off-loaded and re-loaded on to the van. The tears flowed like rivers when I saw the removal men drive away with all my beautifully polished furniture, it was like a bereavement. I had polished everything lovingly for eight years and the sight of them being taken away again was like losing members of my family but I survived. Summer had arrived and Cesar and Ivan soon joined us. Cesar was not sure whether he liked 'Park Place' as much as 'Cherwell'. One day he told me that he rode past our old house to recapture the summer of 1962. Nevertheless the boys soon settled in and I hired bikes for them as usual from a cycle shop in Walton-on-Thames. This shop knew me for years because I always hired bicycles for my foreign children in summer. Cesar had matured and our meeting was a little cold. The atmosphere was different and so were we. 'Park Place' was an elegant little house! I made the brocade curtains in the drawing room and dining room myself. I have always made my own curtains in all my houses except the present one. As I grew older I preferred to buy curtains or get them made because curtain making is a very tedious job. I still enjoy needlework and knitting but since 1986 I have taken up writing as a full-time hobby. I do not intend writing book after book because this is definitely my last one. Everything must end and I feel that this book is the beginning of the end or the end of the beginning of my writing career because I want to spend more time with people. I used to belong to an exercise class at Claygate Day Centre which is run by an ex ballerina who is eighty-two years old. I am thinking of joining the class again in January 2002.

I had three neighbours in 'Park Place' and I introduced the Spanish boys to them and naturally they were all delighted to meet them.

We had many summer parties with music and dancing and Jim Reeves record, 'Welcome to My World' was constantly played. This song has very meaningful words and I like Jim Reeves' voice. My favourite singer is still Frank Sinatra. He had a unique voice, there will never be another singer like Frank! God has taken so many artists to heaven recently I am certain they all have a jolly good time at Christmas. I taught Cesar how to dance the samba to 'Quando, Quando, Quando' so that he could enjoy the parties. At first he was quite nervous but I think that dancing is a very important way of communicating and it is silly if people do not know how to dance when the rhythm changes. My brother and I dance very well together. He is seventy-six-years-old and yet he still goes dancing to The Continental Hotel in Plymouth and why not? I still enjoy Tessa and Gerald's parties, they normally have a marquee in their beautiful garden. Their dinner dances which are usually formal 'Black Tie' functions are well known in our area. It is good to see that they are enjoyed by young and old people. We often have three generations intermingling with one another and a good time is had by everyone.

Richard bought himself a hunting restaurant in Hampstead when we moved into 'Park Place' and since I was not prepared to interrupt the children's education he lived in Hampstead above the restaurant and he only returned on weekends. At first I did not like the idea but I soon got used to it. I am afraid I chose 'motherhood' because bringing up children is a full-time job and entertaining other people's children was a very rewarding occupation.

I shall never forget the tragic story about Cesar's grandfathers! We were having a family lunch on Sunday when Cesar told us that both his grandfathers died in very unusual circumstances.

One fell down the lift shaft and the lift came crashing down on his head and crushed him to death. The other grandfather's chauffeur accidentally stalled his car in the middle of a railway crossing and he was found dead in the back seat still reading his newspaper! I burst out laughing. I excused myself from the table and I went into the kitchen because I was unable to stop laughing. I eventually returned to the dining-room trying desperately hard to keep a straight face. Cesar's expressive account was too much for me and fortunately he broke the icy silence.

'Don't worry Mrs Rumsey we also laugh at these stories. His younger brother Ivan gave me his support as well but Richard, Tessa and Simon were horrified at my behaviour. Latin people have a strange sense of humour because they can laugh at a tragedy and turn it into a comedy. I find some English comedy offensive because it is rude and crude and the jokes do not make me laugh at all. Thank God we are all different as it would be a boring world if we all laughed and cried at the same thing. I had lost my sense of humour until I met Cesar and his brothers again but for the next eight summers I was very happy with these Spanish boys.

'Park Place' did not have the homely atmosphere 'Cherwell' had. The boys all shaved for breakfast unlike 'Cherwell'. One morning Cesar looked as if he had just tumbled out of bed. He never bothered to shave.

'What's wrong with you this morning?' I asked him sternly. But he refused to reply. 'Are you trying to prove to me that you are a man? I can see you haven't shaved' I added and then I began singing. 'At seventeen you fall in love so madly—' as I cooked his bacon and eggs and he played a favourite record of his 'I've Grown Accustomed to Her Face' to calm me down.

I never had a breakfast room in 'Park Place', the whole house had a very formal atmosphere.

Old houses are like old people, they have a hidden charm because they have seen life's joys and sadness but houses cannot write and release a few intimate secrets like I can.

It was during the farewell party I realised that Cesar was deeply interested in my character. He wanted to know more about me so I told him why I got married to Richard. 'I knew something had happened,' he said sympathetically, 'but I also know that you have married the right man for you. Mr Rumsey reminds me of Professor Higgins and you are like Eliza,' he said. He was obviously a deep thinker because I also thought likewise. We took Cesar and Ivan to see *My Fair Lady* in London and Cesar had made up his mind that Richard and I had totally different characters and he was right. Cesar danced with me at the farewell party and I tried to make him feel confident by ignoring the fact that he was trembling with emotion. I do not know how some women can have young lovers because in my eyes it is totally wrong but I do believe that women need to marry men ten years younger than themselves so that we do not have so many widows in old age. Catherine the Great of Russia had an enormous appetite for young lovers, she had a favourite one who was forty years younger than herself. I like young men's company but I would not dream of taking them to bed! I adore flirting and dancing with my grandsons because Grandmothers are no longer 'fuddy-duddies'. We are as I have said before only old children!

Tessa's in-laws and I have a very modern approach to our grandchildren and I think all grandparents have changed for the better.

The summers came and the summers ended as quickly as they began and my life carried on with my highs and lows. I love spring, summer and autumn but I hate winter because I need sunshine throughout the year. Children bring me sunshine on the dullest day!

I became very interested in buying land when I was in 'Park Place' so that Richard could design and build us a home. I found four excellent plots – one in Ashley Road in Walton-on-Thames, one in Burwood Park, one in Ham Court and one on the heath in Weybridge. Richard was too busy with his restaurant at the time so he was only prepared to buy one and he chose to design a house for us on the heath. I would have liked to have bought all four plots because they only cost £5,000 each but Richard was not interested. I had to do all the work – find a builder and raise the finance and I did both myself. The children were growing up and 'Park Place' became too small. I was thinking ahead to the day Tessa and Simon would need a nice home to entertain their friends. I arranged for the builder through an estate agent and the finance was indeed a miracle! I put 'Park Place' up for sale and along came a delightful lady called Mrs Evans with her daughter Jo Jo. Mrs Evans fell in love with the house and she was buying it for her daughter. I met this charming lady through an estate agent and I negotiated the deal with her in the presence of Richard. 'Do you need the house immediately, Mrs Evans?' I asked excitedly.

'No, as a matter of fact I have a nice house in Woking. I am buying this house as an investment for my daughter,' was her amazing reply.

'Can I rent it from you?' I queried and Richard gave me a sharp kick which Mrs Evans saw.

'We do not do business like this in England,' he muttered. But delightful Mrs Evans ignored this ugly outburst and replied sweetly,

'Of course you can.'

'How much do you want for renting the house to me?' I asked.

'How much are you prepared to give me?' she asked hesitatingly.

'£8 a week' I replied.

'Of course you can rent it for £8 a week my dear,' she said smiling at me. 'I have bought the land for £5,000 and I will need a bank loan to start the building,' I told her.

'I shall write you a cheque immediately for £10,500 so you can go ahead with the house,' she said encouragingly. I know nobody would believe this story but this is exactly how I happened to do one of the best transactions I have ever made in front of Richard who was dumbfounded. I never got any thanks for it but I never expected any because Richard was not a businessman.

I bought the land under strange circumstances as well. A spiritualist owned the plot of land which was once part of 'Noirmont', it was actually the ballroom! The dance floor was used in 'Ling Point' but we built 'Noirmont Place' on what was the ballroom. Truth is stranger than fiction. The owner of the stables was selling the land. She had actually sold the land but when I turned up she consulted the spirits who told her to sell the land to me. I could not believe this good fortune. Mrs Waller like Mrs Evans was an elderly widow and she also had a daughter. I think that both these widows treated me like a daughter and they admired my guts. I was going to launch Tessa from 'Noirmont Place'. 'Park Place' by comparison was insignificant. It actually over-looked St George's Hill and my garden sloped into natural woodlands. I remember Cesar visiting me when I had purchased the land and we both walked through the overgrown woodlands talking about my plans. 'You will always get what you want,' remarked Cesar. How wrong he was or I should say how right Tessa was to make her own plans as to who she would marry. I have to admit that at one time I wanted Tessa to marry Cesar but it was not to be and neither of us regret it.

Ode to Noirmont Place

Noirmont Place was built by a gentleman builder called Mr Gosden. The building trade was going through a bad patch at the time and we were very lucky to get this thoroughly honest builder who built us a four bedroom home for next to nothing in comparison to today's prices. Again luck played a great deal in this mammoth task. It was one of the most exciting periods of my life seeing our home come up brick by brick.

I often took Tessa and Simon to view their future home after school and Snow Boy, our adorable white poodle, loved to run in the woods. I can still smell the beautiful tall pine trees!

We had a lovely mature copper beach tree and many colourful rhododendrons which grew wild. It really was a shame to cultivate the land and turn part of it into a garden and leave part woodlands. We had an exquisite magnolia tree which burst into flower in spring every year looking like a radiant bride! I often compared Tessa to this beautiful tree and I thank God she left 'Noirmont Place' as a bride married to a middle class well-educated Ampleforth boy. I could not imagine this happening in 'Park Place'. My son-in-law Gerald comes from a very good family. One of Gerald's ancestors was made a Lord because he fought for the crown against Lily Langtree and he was knighted. I sometimes feel like Lily Langtree but nobody bothers to fight for or against me now. I do not know how I exist because everyone seems to have forgotten how much I did for them. There is a saying that behind every successful man there is a woman and I would like to add that behind every successful woman there is herself! Times have changed and mothers are no longer considered to be like jewels which can never be replaced. Husbands and wives take priority over mothers now and they wake up too late when they find themselves in an old people's home amongst strangers. I am dreading this experience and I *must* resist this happening at all costs.

We moved into 'Noirmont Place' in the summer of 1966. Ivan spent the summer with us that year and I remember Cesar writing him a letter telling him how much he was missing his summer holidays in England. He was doing his National Service that summer and when he heard 'Smoke Gets in Your Eyes' he thought of the happy times he had spent with our family. 'Give my best wishes to Mrs Rumsey,' he wrote.

Ivan read Cesar's letter out to me. Ivan was a different character to Cesar. He was a playboy who enjoyed smoking, he was undoubtedly the rebel in the family. I liked Ivan but I liked all Cesar's brothers. Germain was very studious, he was also very different to his two elder brothers but Julio, who was the youngest brother was very charming. He looked quite English but none of Cesar's brothers had their eldest brother's confident personality. He was self assured at sixteen! I suppose being the eldest son of an important banking family made Cesar grow up before his time. I remember meeting the eldest son of a famous Greek shipping company in Calcutta when I worked in a Dutch shipping office. He took me out one night to The Grand Hotel and we got caught in the pouring rain. My pretty chiffon dress was drenched! This handsome young man invited me to his room in The Grand Hotel in order to get it pressed. I innocently fell for this invitation because we were going dancing to Princes. I slipped my dress off and he handed it to a porter. I sat on the bed in my petticoat and quite naturally the charming Greek lay me back tenderly on the bed to make love to me. I was taken by surprise and I foolishly burst into tears! He felt an awful heel. 'Let's go dancing to Princes,' he said coaxingly. 'I'm sorry if I have offended you but I cannot bear tears,' he said brushing them away. My tears have always come to my rescue in an awkward situation. We did go dancing to Princes. I told Richard about the Greek and I was not surprised to see Richard with his friend Syd at Princes as well. I did go out with other friends at the beginning of my courtship with Richard and he accepted it because we were not engaged. I also went out with a handsome young Frenchman. Bob invited me to his apartment but he did not dare to touch me. When I think back on it poor Bob had soft romantic background music playing. He reclined on his bed in his bedsit and I sat on a chair in the corner of the room. This romantic encounter must have been a kind of well-planned seduction but again I was foolishly unaware of it at the time. I was enjoying the music and I thought that Bob was as well.

I was quite surprised when he suddenly got up from his reclining posture and said, 'You better stay with Richard because he will marry you.' He took me back to the YWCA and we parted good friends.

I enjoyed going on Bob's fast motorbike and when our brief relationship came to an end I was very upset. Richard was the first man who invited me to his apartment and I was scared because I had been warned by my mother never to do this. I trusted Richard because Mary had chosen him for me and when our friendship became more intimate I also walked into his bedroom. Lovemaking in my day did not involve intercourse. It must have been very frustrating from the man's point of view and had I known how it was going to end I would never have attempted sex. But I know that Richard and I have never regretted having our two children. We both loved Tessa and Simon very much and neither of us would be without them. It is children who cement a relationship and I am sure many 'shot-gun' marriages have turned out better than couples living together for years and then divorcing one another in marriage. I am now a proud grandmother of ten grandchildren. Unfortunately Richard did not live long enough to see the grandchildren growing up like I have. I hope that one day all families will be reunited in heaven where there will be no more sad partings.

Tessa spent the summer of 1967 in Spain with Cesar's family in Santander. If nothing else it taught Tessa how the other half of the world lives. Tessa is very rich in her own right because Gerald has been a marvellous husband to my daughter. He has given her great wealth and happiness. Cesar and Gerald met briefly one night at 'Noirmont Place.' I remember telling Cesar that Gerald would marry Tessa one day but his pride would not accept it. I remember him saying 'Gerald is no competition!' How wrong he was.

Tessa was sixteen years old when she spent three months with Cesar's family and on 11 December this year it was Tessa and

Gerald's twenty-fifth wedding anniversary. How time flies! Marriages are made in heaven and arranged marriages will soon be a thing of the past because young Indian people living in England will not accept their parents' choice. I had no right to influence Tessa to marry Cesar and looking back on this now I am glad that Tessa made her own choice and everything has worked out well for Cesar as well. He married a marquis' daughter and he has a large family of his own. I sometimes wish that Cesar's children could get a chance to meet Tessa's children because I am still a romantic matchmaker at heart! I love my twenty-one-year-old granddaughter Sophie very much and I sometimes wonder who she will marry. Sweet Sophie is very beautiful and she deserves a Prince Charming! I think that her boyfriend Danny is the right person for her so I must not start matchmaking again. It is not up to Tessa or I to decide the children's future. I am certain that all my grandchildren will find someone who will love and appreciate them because they are all lovely children.

Twenty-five years ago Tessa married Gerald and it was twenty-five years ago that I got my first breakdown. My world fell apart when Tessa left home because we were great friends. When Tessa and Gerald went to Bahrain with their baby son I fell to pieces because Simon moved into Tessa's house in Shepherds Bush. I encouraged Simon to make this move because Tessa found Mr Right when she moved into an apartment in London with a couple of girlfriends and I felt sure that Simon would also do likewise. Simon did find his first wife Suzy as soon as he moved into Tessa's house in Shepherd's Bush and Suzy moved in as well. Both my children have launched themselves! At this time Richard's restaurant in Hampstead was becoming a financial burden. Richard had problems of his own and I could not do anything to help him.

This is when I started taking tranquillisers which sent me into a deep depression. I had looked after Mary and Norine who both landed up with psychiatrists and I never thought that I would do likewise. I can only blame it on our tragic background. We were orphans stranded in India with no parents. Since we all married Englishmen, except Olive, our new homes were in England. The English way of life is vastly different to India and both these fragile sisters could not cope with it. I was responsible for sending Norine to England because she was the only unmarried sister and she met her English husband who was in the Malayan Police Force on her way to England. It was a boardship romance! Jim was a divorced man with three children of his own. He was a very nice man but he was unable to find a decent job in England on his return from Malaya. Poor Norine was unable to cope with her financial troubles and she lived in a caravan in the end with Jim and their two children. This dilemma would have sent me round the bend! Norine was the lead singer in the family. She should have continued her singing career because she was unable to cope with marriage and motherhood. Fortunately the whole family immigrated to Australia where the weather is warmer. Norine is also a widow and she lives in an old people's home in Sydney. Her children are very good to her and she seems to be very content with her life. Norine has never wanted material things in her life. She used to share a bedroom with me and I had to do everything for her. I thought she was very brave to do the long sea voyage alone. When I saw her fragile figure disappear I waved until she was out of sight with the tears rolling down my cheeks. Unfortunately I had to send her to Mary until I arrived with Richard. These two sisters never got on because they were very alike. They both had boyfriends from an early age unlike Olive, Lynnette and myself who listened to our precious mother. Norine married Jim when I was in Hampstead. I bought her her wedding outfit and she flew out to Kuala Lumpur where Jim was in the police force. If Mary and Norine had lived abroad all their lives I am certain neither of them would have got mentally ill.

Both these sisters needed to be waited on. Norine's husband did all the domestic chores for her but Mary's husband was a bully. He made sure he was waited on and Mary's illness has lasted a lifetime. She is a schizophrenic who hears voices like I hear a ringing noise in my head. I do not know if schizophrenia is an imaginary illness so I cannot account for the voices. The ringing noise in my head is due to drugs but arthritis also plays a major role because my creative brain has to be kept alive and many people suffer from noises in their heads. I suppose it is a small price to pay for life!

I became very creative when I was given Oestrogen in 1982. I wrote three books in the space of a year in order to try to recover Richard's financial losses. I got the inspiration to write in Positano in Italy. I remember standing on the balcony on a wonderful starry night admiring the beautiful scenery, the dramatic cliffs plunged into a deep blue sea. The water was crystal clear and I was actually interested to learn how to swim! Richard hired a car and we visited Rome, Pompeii and Vesuvius. We also went by boat to Capri and visited the Blue Lagoon which was a very beautiful sight. I had a very amusing incident which happened on the beach one day when Tessa and I were sitting on a wall. A young Italian and his English girlfriend had been observing us and in the end her Italian boyfriend beckoned us over to his table. I pointed to Tessa thinking he wanted to meet her but he made a joke of it and said 'No, I want to meet you as well. I will give you some ice cream!' I burst out laughing because I was forty-nine years old and I found it rather amusing to be wooed with ice-cream! We did join this young couple and they invited us to a lovely night club. I enjoyed dancing with this young man who was a marvellous dancer. I had a very painful left knee at the time and dancing was a good way of releasing the stiffness. I still resort to dancing to ease the pain and stiffness. We also went to a wonderful night club called the Africano in Amalfi.

This club was situated in a cave by the sea and we were able to see the sea rushing in and out under the dance floor! The Italians certainly know how to enjoy life to the full and we spent a marvellous holiday in Positano which gave me the inspiration to write a book.

Ode to Holloway Sanatorium

My private consultant endocrinologist in London gave me a pill to help me sleep at night which had the opposite effect. I had phoned my GP several times during the night because I was taking more and more pills. 'I shall see you tomorrow. No more pills,' he told me several times. On thinking logically about it I should have sent for an ambulance so that I could be admitted into hospital. Nevertheless I survived until the following morning and my GP brought a psychiatrist to the house. I think he was shocked to see my state because I looked haggard and I had lost my voice completely. He summed up the situation immediately. 'Look at your wife,' he told Richard. 'Is this the woman you married?' he asked him. Then he spoke to Tessa and Simon 'Is this your mother?' he asked again.

'I would like to go into hospital,' I pleaded but he did not agree.

'I can give you your medication at home. You have a lovely home and I am reluctant to admit you into hospital, you will not like it,' he told me. He gave me a drug called Haluperidol and Arctane which had a horrific effect on me. I dreamt I was being orbited into space and I woke up screaming my prayers! The following morning I was unable to walk so another consultant psychiatrist admitted me into Holloway Sanatorium in Virginia Water because there was nobody to look after me at home. Richard was in Hampstead, Tessa was on her way to Bahrain and Simon had moved into Tessa's house in Shepherd's Bush. I had no alternative but to go into hospital.

Holloway Sanatorium in Virginia Water had once been a stately home so on first impressions it looked like a nice place. But when I was shown my cubicle which resembled a prison cell because the tiny window had bars on it I became alarmed. The dreadful hard bed had paper sheets on it because my room had a burst pipe and the bed linen was soaked. Richard dropped me off and when he left I soon realised why my consultant psychiatrist was not keen to admit me. We had one small stuffy reception room which was filled with smoke because all the inmates were chain smokers, I have never indulged in this bad habit. I found this meeting place unbearable because there were all sorts of people from various backgrounds thrown together. One day a young lady appeared in a glamorous fur coat singing at the top of her voice. I heard that she was a schizophrenic. Poor Mary and Norine were labelled schizophrenics but neither of them are violent, and Norine never heard voices.

The following morning I had the courage to go to the dining room for breakfast. I was surprised to find that this room was a palatial one. On the surface 'Holloway Sanatorium' appeared to be a well run hospital but the wards where the patients slept and lived were barbaric! I remember spending my last night in an over-crowded tiny room with the smell of unwashed bodies lying around. It is this disgraceful 'behind the scenes' atmosphere that *must* be revealed. I had an excellent breakfast but I had to make a quick exit when a patient approached me.

'I am going to do you in,' he threatened. I was very frightened so I returned to the ward and I reported him to Armenia, who was the ward sister. I still remember her name. 'Don't worry, he will not be able to do a thing because he is heavily sedated,' she assured me.

I shall never forget Holloway Sanatorium for as long as I live! The sinister tower still dominates the sky line.

It always brings back bad memories for Tessa and I. My beloved daughter brought her baby son James to say 'goodbye' because she was off to Bahrain and she changed his nappy on my bed. I was ashamed to be in a mental hospital but at that time I had no choice. I am pleased to say that my consultant psychiatrist was happy to discharge me in a week. I have been in psychiatric care for twenty-eight years but my depression was only successfully treated in 1986. I was given a potent drug called Amitriptyline which hit the musical area of my brain and I got a loud ringing noise in my head which I still have today. This experienced psychiatrist had channelled my creative brain. I believe I tick from the same area as all the great writers! He told me that it is in my best interests to write. Amitriptyline and Prozac heated up my ice cold body. Previously I have no idea how I survived the English winters because I should have died of hypothermia years ago! I did get hot flushes after my hysterectomy but when they subsided my body became like a block of ice and my kidneys stopped functioning. I went to my GP and he sent me to a consultant endocrinologist in London who treated me with Thyroxine for many years. I took 300 mcgs of Thyroxine for many years which could be responsible for my depression.

I left Holloway Sanatorium no better than when I entered. I was prescribed Dalmane and an old-fashioned anti-depressant called Prondol. Neither of these drugs helped and the terrible cough returned. Psychiatrists have a very difficult job to diagnose a case because the brain is an inexact organ.

I like psychiatrists but they should remember that every patient is an individual and they must try to understand why we are as we are. We are all God's creatures – a queen bee is a queen bee and a worker is a worker. I am undoubtedly a worker bee. That's life!

Ode to The Abraham Cowley Unit

My second nervous breakdown followed a few years later. My grandchildren James and Sophie were children and not babies anymore. Everything was going wrong in my life. Tessa and Simon had left home and Richard's restaurant was in serious financial trouble. Richard never discussed his business problems with anyone which was a big mistake. His father was very hard on him when he was a boy but he did not realise that I was always willing to help him. I knew Richard had no lease left on the restaurant so he had nothing to sell. It was very foolish to run a restaurant without a lease and when I heard he was borrowing vast sums of money from the bank I became worried. 'What are you using for collateral?' I asked him one day. 'Noirmont Place' was his frank reply. 'Not the roof over my head, Hubba! I have worked so hard to get this house for you and the children. Not our home. You can borrow the money from the two properties we have in Albert Road in Bournemouth,' I suggested. I was relieved when he agreed to do this instead. Meanwhile I continued to visit psychiatrists in order to be able to cope with the situation. I remember meeting a young well-educated Indian psychiatrist who was on a six-month work permit in England. I still remember his name but since this is a true story I am not going to mention any doctors' names. This psychiatrist never spoke a word to me for a couple of minutes and suddenly he plucked up the courage to ask the ridiculous question, 'Do you hear voices?' he asked sheepishly.

'No, except when you spoke to me just now,' I replied. We eventually had a normal discussion. I gave him a brief family history telling him I was born and lived in India for twenty-eight years and I soon realised we had a good rapport. It is most important for me to have an immediate bond with a doctor otherwise I will not take the medication. I told him that my father had worked for the Maharaja of Holkar as a Conservator of Forests which made him prescribe a pill.

Bolvidon had a very undesirable effect on me. I got severe palpitation and I had to be admitted into The Abraham Cowley Unit. Sometimes psychiatrists seem to deliberately prescribe a potent pill in order to admit us into hospital where they can monitor our medication.

When one is admitted into The Abraham Cowley Unit it is like going to a pantomime! I did not know who was the doctor and who was the patient. In my opinion the doctors and patients both appear to be very highly strung people. I am a good spectator in times of crisis so I decided to write a short pantomime about a mental hospital. I made the senior consultant psychiatrist into a magnificent lion because this doctor had beautiful silver hair and a beard, but another patient said he looked like a garden gnome! I described the young Indian doctor as a loveable walrus. I turned an enormous psychiatrist into an elephant. It was a very amusing piece of work. I expect the Indian doctor thought because my father was a Conservator of Forests I knew all about animals! I have come to realise over the years that psychiatry is a trial and error business; it is a kind of guessing game. Perhaps it is amusing for psychiatrists but if they were the patients they would know how it feels to have one's brain bombarded with potent drugs. I had been given twenty-five different antidepressants for my depression and it was only removed in 1986 when I was given an old-fashioned pill which is no longer used anymore. This experienced psychiatrist moved the depression but I have to live with the consequences – the unbearable ringing noises in my head! I met my daily help when I was admitted into Clare Ward. I was the only person who could communicate with Christine who was in a deep depression and so was I. I managed to persuade her to help me to wash the medicine glasses. I did the wash up and Christine dried them. It was like old times again! Christine was a splendid worker.

She got a breakdown because her young daughter pinched her boyfriend. It came as a big surprise to her. Christine's boyfriend was an elderly man. She gave him all his meals and she did all his washing for him as well. Her silly daughter cheated on her mother, the man was old enough to be her father! I think that Christine's depression was caused by sleeping pills because my depression started when I took them as well. Unfortunately I have to take sleeping pills at night in order to knock the loud ringing noise out of my head!

When I was in the Abraham Cowley Unit the drugs were changed quite frequently and because I got a dreadful cough simple linctus was given to me at night which did not help at all. I met a consultant psychiatrist socially through a friend, he was her father-in-law. He had worked in Epsom Mental Hospital and he told me that even though he retired many years ago he still wakes up in the middle of the night in a cold sweat when he thinks of the barbaric treatment mentally ill patients were given many years ago.

I am glad that I am now being treated for blood pressure which is more serious than depression because the consequences can be disastrous. My GP is still keen for me to see a psychiatrist because she thinks I am depressed. But in spite of my depression I have managed to write an interesting autobiography on a blood pressure pill! I do not want to return to psychiatrists again. Modern antidepressants are fast acting but unfortunately they have to be constantly changed.

When I was discharged from The Abraham Cowley Unit my depression returned. Unfortunately I could not tolerate Amitriptyline which was later changed to Prozac.

Ode to Richard's Return

My highs and lows continued for several years but I did have a good reason to be depressed. Richard had closed his restaurant and it was terribly sad to see him return home in a hired van with all his pots and pans including his good quality china and cutlery. My heart bled for him! He knew that this would happen one day so when that day arrived it did not come as a surprise. I welcomed him home and we both made plans to sell 'Noirmont Place' in the near future and move into a smaller house.

Richard and I had not lived together for many years and I know nothing about his life in Hampstead. I shall undoubtedly know something more about it on Friday, 28 December. I had a strange telephone call from a man a few days ago asking to speak to Mr Rumsey. This telephone call came as a big shock to me and I had to tell the man the sad news 'Mr Rumsey died in 1991. I am his wife,' I told him.

'I'm sorry to hear Richard popped his clogs,' he replied.

'Who are you?' I queried inquisitively.

'My name is Charles Petters. Richard and I have been very good friends for forty-eight years. I have just returned from New Zealand with my daughter,' he told me.

'Where do you live?' I asked.

'I live in Richmond. I would like to meet you over the holiday period. Would Friday the 28th be convenient for me to call?' he queried.

'Yes, I look forward to meeting you,' I said excitedly.

'I'll call around 11 a.m.,' he replied.

'That's fine. I shall expect you on the 28th,' I told him.

Before he hung up he told me, 'You are a very lucky lady to have been married to such a handsome charismatic man like Richard. He had many friends in Hampstead. He was a very intelligent interesting man who was well-liked by everybody,' he said.

The conversation was about to end so I asked him 'Did Richard ever talk about me?'

'Yes, he often mentioned you and we all agreed that you were a lucky lady to have a husband like Richard,' he replied.

I only saw Richard once a week. He returned home late on a Saturday night and he went back to Hampstead on Monday morning. I once had a very happy personality like a Koh-in-Noor diamond but the loneliness turned me into a solitaire! I have bought myself a solitaire ring for Christmas and it now sparkles for me on my old arthritic hand. I become very depressed when I hear this sad song but who knows I might find friendship with Charles who is 81 years old? If he is anything like Richard he will be 81 years young! I cannot believe this meeting is going to take place on Friday. My readers and I will have to wait and see what happens. God does work in mysterious ways!

Ode to Hanover Walk

We sold 'Noirmont Place' on 28 June 1984. It was a devastating experience for me because I was really responsible for building the house. Richard only designed it but I handled the finance for all the stage payments etc. from start to finish. It was difficult to walk out of a house I had put on the map of Weybridge!

My life is very different in Hanover Walk because I share a roof with five other people. I told Richard that I would hate to buy a semi-detached house because I do not like sharing a roof with anyone. Roof trouble can be a serious problem. I sometimes see 'roofers' doing work in Hanover Walk which could be very expensive.

Everyone keeps to themselves here. My mother-in-law gave me a piece of advice. 'Never make friends with your immediate neighbours,' she told me. But I do not entirely agree.

I am glad I have made friends with Fi because she is a charming Asian girl. My South African lodger came into my life when both of us needed one another most so I am not lonely now. God looks after me in a very special way and He sends people into my life when I need them. We all have a different hobby in life. Some people play bridge to fill the lonely hours but I need lodgers from all parts of the world to brighten my days.

When Richard and I moved into Hanover Walk a great family friend wanted to be our lodger. He was originally going to live with his son and daughter-in-law but his plans fell through. This great friend was our retired bank manager and he played a major part in our lives. He was a very good man, and had been a widower for many years and he came to our assistance when we were in financial difficulties. I remember asking him for a bank loan.

'I promise to pay it back in a few months,' I told him and his reply gave me great confidence to go ahead with my plans.

'I very often believe a woman more than a man,' he remarked with a twinkle in his eyes! He was a Mason and one of the masonic good works is to take care of widows. I had been a widow, more or less, for many years when Richard lived in Hampstead and this kind man befriended me. He gave Tessa a reference for a job and most importantly he launched Simon's business. He also told me, 'Do not stop writing because you have a unique style. You remind me of Alice in Wonderland but one day you will be appreciated. I have seen it happen many times before.' I hope this dear friend's words will come true one day because I know he believed in me. I looked after him for four and a half years and they were my happiest years because I had no financial worries.

When my retired bank manager came to live with us Richard could not wait to run away. It was clear to see that he wanted to move on. He was obviously missing his bachelor life in Hampstead.

Richard once told me that he would like to live in Istanbul! He was a wanderer and Hanover Walk was not his cup of tea. We had a silly argument one day at lunch and he stormed up to his room packed his suitcase and he told me 'I'm leaving you.' I retaliated with very cruel words like a 'she devil' which came to pass.

Richard found it very difficult to find suitable lodgings after home comforts. He told me that the houses were dirty and the beds had bugs in them. In despair he bought himself a delightful narrow boat called 'Rosy' which he converted into a lovely home. We still kept in touch with one another and I soon realised that

'Rosy' was the new woman in his life! Simon gave Richard a job in Artel Communications so he was not short of money. I was also generous to him because I gave him an attractive red Lancia car. It was a sporty little car but I found it difficult to drive. I bought myself a Fiat Uno instead because I only need a car to get me to Waitrose and back. I am not a long distance driver like Richard.

Richard had a terrible disaster one year at Christmas. He returned home one day to find that 'Rosy' had sunk! All his hard work including his possessions were at the bottom of the canal. He got in touch with me because he needed some money to salvage 'Rosy' and I was only too pleased to help him out. I do not know how Richard had the guts to restore 'Rosy' again to her former glory but he did it and I was proud to help him out financially in this mammoth task. Richard was a young boy at heart and because I have a motherly character our marriage survived. We were always united in times of a crisis and I still long for him to turn up unexpectedly. It was my depressive illness that drove him away and I do not blame him for leaving me. I cannot live with myself when I am depressed because my real character is a very happy one but like 'Rosy' I can sink into the depths of despair. I do not want to sink again because Richard is not around to salvage me!

Richard became very ill in 1987 and he was diagnosed as having cancer of the prostrate gland. He had an emergency operation but unfortunately the surgeon was unable to do anything so he had to have a colostomy. I was shattered to hear this bad news when I visited him in hospital. He battled bravely with his illness for two and a half years. In a way God sent him home to me at last and I was able to look after him until he died. His bravery was incredible. He took up French polishing as a hobby and he worked long hours in the garage polishing the family furniture.

At this tragic time my retired bank manager's health was also failing. I looked after two terminally ill men single handed for two and a half years not knowing who would die first. My retired bank manager died of a massive heart attack in 1989 and Richard died in 1991. During this period I was in charge of Richard's medication and I was amazed at my capability. I did my job with courage and dignity. I never went near a psychiatrist because my GP gave me the necessary medication to look after Richard until the bitter end. Fortunately I had one good lodger living with us who stood silently behind me. I lost two important men in my life one after the other but life carries on through my wonderful children and grandchildren. Whenever I get lonely I get in touch with my daughter and her lovely family.

Ode to The White House

It was good to pop into 'The White House' yesterday which was as usual full of *life*. 'Put the kettle on Mummy,' said my daughter Tessa as she continued to speak in fluent French with her daughter Kate in order to help her with her French homework.

Little Emma appeared to be stressed out, she was harassing her mother because she was in one of her 'whingeing' moods but as usual Tessa handled her youngest daughter firmly but kindly. How does my daughter stretch herself in so many directions at the same time? She has to in order to cope with her demanding family.

Tessa has five children, one boy and four girls. It amazes me to see that my little girl has become a very capable wife, mother and 'Jill of all Trades!' The ever-increasing laundry had to be sorted out and bulbs and winter pansies were waiting to be planted by her and yet she never forgot to give her husband Gerald his cup of tea. Gerald, like Tessa, was busy working sorting out some mechanical parts on a table in the garden.

When Emma's 'whingeing' became unbearable Gerald soon put a stop to it. 'What's all this noise about Emma?' he asked. 'If you continue to worry Mummy I will get very angry with you and then I will give you a smack,' he added sternly. Meanwhile, Emma had rolled herself into a ball behind the dining room door and she was laughing hysterically when her father barged into the room. I was standing beside her, trying to calm her down by telling her that she was lucky to have a nice Daddy because when I was young I only had cruel nuns!

My grandchildren's lives are very different from mine when I was a child. We had very little family life because my widowed mother packed her five daughters and only son off to boarding school in the hills for nine months of the year from the age of seven to seventeen. The girls were sent to convents so we were brought up by nuns and my brother was brought up by Christian brothers. It was this lack of home life which accounted for the tragedies that were to follow in later life. However in spite of all our troubles the six of us are still alive today because we are survivors.

Later on in the afternoon Kate decided to play her saxophone and she put her French homework aside. Kate, who is sixteen, is a brilliant musician. She played a tape of South American music and belted out some of her grandmother's favourite tunes on her saxophone. I love South American music and dancing; something our family have inherited from our Portuguese father. He sadly died of a stroke at the age of forty-two when I was only eighteen months old. My father left us with his talent for music and yesterday, like many other days in the distant past, I came alive for a brief moment in 'The White House' and I actually got up and danced for Kate.

I have been in a black tunnel of depression for months but I have refused to take any more antidepressants which act as a 'quick fix' for a while so I am now being treated for high blood pressure. My future is black but I know that it can become rosy again if I begin to appreciate music. I may even write another book which will pull me through the winter. I am a bored seventy-eight-year-old grandmother! I can still live a colourful life through my children and grandchildren but I have to smile.

People change on the surface as they grow older but we still remain the same. When I look into the mirror I can see that my image is old but behind the physical ageing is a hidden personality which can sparkle like a diamond!

Yes, in my mind I am still that breathless teenager of seventeen struggling to get out to enjoy what is left of the rest of my life. I am not afraid of death, it is living a life of hell here on earth that frightens me.

Sunday is the loneliest day of the week when one is a widow but today Tessa has invited me to lunch at 2 p.m. I am glad we are having a late lunch because I have been busy writing all morning.

I usually write my books off the cuff when I am on an anti-depressants because the words chase one another very quickly but this morning I have had to do three drafts. Lunch on a Sunday at 'The White House' is a grand affair because we usually have it in the elegant dining room and Tessa cooks us an excellent meal. Now that winter is approaching I may enjoy a Sunday roast every weekend if I smile! Today we had roast lamb, roast potatoes and broccoli cooked to perfection, followed by tasty tarts which Tessa's in-laws brought back from a holiday in Lisbon, they were delicious. I helped with the washing up of the cooking utensils and everything else went in the dishwasher. I also made the coffee so if I keep up this good behaviour Sunday can once again be the happiest day of the week.

Tessa is my eldest child, but I also have a son called Simon, he is four years younger than his sister. Simon lives in Oxshott and his beautiful home is called 'Eastwood House'. Both of my children are a great credit to me. My life has been a 'Comedy of Errors' but my late husband, Richard and my two children have been the best investments I ever had.

Previous to my marriage I was a vain little flirt, attracting many admirers because my motto was 'Why make one man miserable when you can make many happy?' It was the men who did the flirting by winking at me and I blew them kisses. I have no idea how Richard put up with this Latin behaviour! I have my father's personality or perhaps I am like his Spanish mother?

My mother's father was English and her mother was Irish but I also have a sprinkling of Dutch, because my maternal grandmother was a Maisie Van Dort. I got a job in KLM when I was a young girl because my maiden name is Alberts. My father and his brother changed their surnames at Rotterdam when they boarded a ship to the Far East.

When my brother was demobbed from the RAF in London he emigrated to Rhodesia to work in the Copper Mines and everyone thought that he was Dutch. Today nobody bothers about ancestors but I do believe we inherit our personalities from them and there is nothing we can do about it.

My family have always been great travellers and today I have two sisters in Sydney Australia and one in America. My brother and eldest sister live in Devon and I live in Weybridge, near my daughter who has the best house in the road. I love 'The White House' but I would never like to own it. I like popping in and out to enjoy the atmosphere. The house is magnificent and the garden is beautiful. I do not need to go to Wisley Gardens like many OAP's because I can sit on a nice swing seat and watch my grandchildren frolicking about in their lovely swimming pool and gaze at the stars on a summer's night, dreaming my loneliness away. I sometimes think about the days when moonlight, music and romance were so important for me. I live in an elegant town house, very near my daughter and yet at times she seems so near and yet so far because I do not want to invade her space.

Tessa is an extremely busy lady because she has three homes to look after. She has a holiday home in Aldeburgh because the family enjoy sailing, a London apartment and 'The White House.' In addition to her own children, there are numerous children's friends. I sometimes compare Tessa's kitchen to Waterloo Station! There is also a party room which has an en suite shower, etc. at the bottom of the garden, near the swimming pool, where the children can have their own parties and sleep over guests.

What a privileged life! Gerald and Tessa are very good parents and they have given their children a wonderful childhood.

Gerald, like my husband Richard, is a very good handyman. They both took an interest in carpentry in their public schools, which is a most useful hobby. Sometimes, when I am sitting on my favourite swing seat in the garden, I admire the tree house Gerald made with his daughter Lucy, high up in an old oak tree. Gerald is a man of great stamina, he is a 'Jack of all Trades' and a master of all! Lucy got her tree house in the end but, now that the children are growing up, they do not use it as often as they did but I still appreciate all the hard work that went into it. I admire my son-in-law's character, he is a good husband, an excellent father and a very kind son-in-law who accepts me as I am. I have a marvellous rapport with him, unlike most mothers-in-law, who are treated like dragons.

It is a glorious Autumn day, brilliant sunshine with no hint of rain. We have been having heavy downpours recently, similar to the monsoon in Calcutta. The climate seems to be changing in England because Autumn can be compared to an Indian summer. October is a very special month for me because I was born on the 28 October 1923, when a pretty girl was like a melody!

I was born in a Nursing Home run by Catholic nuns in Indore. I know that most people are born indoors but Indore is a town in Central India. If you look at a map, you will find that Indore is almost in the centre of the vast continent. I always compare my place of birth to India's beating heart! It is not a well-known town like Bombay, Calcutta or Madras but it is important to me.

My father was very disappointed that I was not a boy because he was looking for a companion who would one day accompany him on tiger shoots etc.

Ironically he gave me his hazel eyes which my mother described were like an Autumn leaf!

'You know my darling, your father's eyes had the greenness of spring, the brownness of summer and the rich multi-colours of an autumn leaf; there was no winter there,' she exclaimed wistfully. Perhaps this is why he swept my English mother off her feet and married her after a brief courtship. His love letters also played a big part in this passionate romance.

Eyes are most important to see with but hands are also important. They are used for work and, above all, for welcoming and greeting a person. My husband once told me that my fingers were like the petals of a flower. He should see them now, they look like ugly, knotted twigs! A psychiatrist once described me as a highly strung, pedigree race-horse, but if he saw me now he would call me a donkey! My shoulders which are also very important are dropping, especially the left one. It was those off-the-shoulder evening gowns I wore when I was a young woman that I am being punished for now. Like Princess Diana, I always exposed my shoulders, especially the left one which is most painful now. There is no hell, it is here on earth and we must all grin and bear it. I remember Diana saying in a tragic interview on the TV,' I will not go quietly...' Neither will I. I am determined to get at least one of my fourteen attempts to write a book published.

I am like a spider weaving my last web! I have one in the garden at the moment: this amazing creature has made a most intricate web from my clothes line to the exotic Yucca plant which is still in bloom. I have not got the heart to destroy it but because this book is a true story I popped out into the garden a moment ago but there was no spider and no web. The horrible monsoon rain must have destroyed it. Nature is so cruel but human beings are worse. Animals eat one another because they are hungry but human beings use destructive weapons to kill innocent people and then try and say that it was God's will.

It was not God but the devil who destroyed the twin towers in America. It is not necessary to go to church to pray devoutly on one's knees several times a day – that won't get us to heaven, it is the way we treat one another that will decide who goes to heaven or hell. If we all loved our neighbours like ourselves we would not need to have these unnecessary wars.

I am feeling happy today because my Greek girlfriend phoned me from Athens to tell me that she will be arriving in England on Saturday. Julie and I have been great friends for many years. We met one another at a rather dull coffee morning. As soon as Julie arrived in her colourful clothes, glittering with jewels, she cheered up the party and we became good friends. I now call her my 'sunshine friend' because she usually brings good weather with her. Today has been a nice bright, sunny day and I hope that the next fortnight will be sunny as well because Julie and I hate the cold, grey days in England.

I met my best friend June in a very strange way. I was taking a short walk down Oatlands Drive, when I saw a tiny lady with a beautiful Lurcher on the lead cross the road and walk away from me. She had a very elegant carriage, she was small but she held her head up high. I was writing *Swan Songs* at the time so I was in a very creative mood. I stopped and stared at June and willed her to cross back to my side of the road so that we would meet because I felt sure she was born in India. Now this is where God comes in. I am certain He read my thoughts and June immediately crossed the road again and we met face to face on the same pavement. She smiled at me but I did the talking as usual, 'I have been watching you,' I said, trying to make friends. June stopped and smiled again so I continued to break the ice.

'I willed you to cross the road again so that we could meet one another.' I asked excitedly, 'Were you born in India?'

'As a matter of fact, I was,' she replied in her posh English accent!

'I knew you were by the way you walked,' I added confidently. 'What's your name?'

'June,' she replied, still bemused at this strange encounter.

'Oh! You're June in January,' I said breaking into song. 'Forgive me, you must think I'm mad but I'm writing a book at the moment. Where do you live?'

'In Bournemouth,' she replied.

'No, I mean where do you live in Weybridge?'

'Not far from here. I am staying with my daughter at the moment.' And so it came to pass that June's daughter was living practically opposite Tessa's house!

God knows that I only write books because I am so lonely, sometimes I am lonely in a crowd and the only way I can communicate with people is by writing.

It is 7 p.m. and I have just heard the thunder and seen a flash of lightning and now it is pouring with rain. Perhaps the rain drops are falling like pennies from heaven to encourage me to hit the jackpot with my last book. My brave spider has missed tonight's downpour. I want to cry for her because she must be homeless now but worse things are happening to innocent people in Afghanistan, who are living rough in tents. Human beings are worse than animals! I sincerely hope that God will forgive us all for what we sometimes accidentally do to one another. I am by no means a saint because, like Mary Magdalen, I am a sinner but I never forget Christ's words on the cross, 'Father forgive them for they know not what they do.' I did not know what was being done to me for years and years. 'I have got to knock your brain out in order to make your body function,' I was told by a famous consultant endocrinologist. 'Your brain does not accept the normal functions of life,' he added. The brain is man's greatest asset and my brain does accept the important functions of life.

I love people who love people. I am a very caring person and, if I had my way, I would like to change the world, not myself. I want to break down all barriers and make human beings realise that we all need one another.

My beloved son phoned me tonight from his car on his way home to tell me that he will be coming to see me with the children on Saturday. I adore my son and yet I gave him away twice to women who do not appreciate him. I often want to snatch him back and scream, 'He's mine!' I have a marvellous rapport with Simon because he is like me – a born romantic. Tessa has her father's character and she has often told me, 'Mummy, life's a bitch and then you die,' and I want to add, 'Please tell me why?'

Tell me why the world is round and yet all nations are divided? I wrote a beautiful poem in 1982 on the question, 'Tell me why?' Now I am searching for the answers. I know why I burnt my first book that was 405 pages long and so does Tessa. It was her cruel words, 'Mummy, let's face it you cannot write a book,' she told me when she found me crying by the huge bonfire of all my hard work and yet psychiatrists have told me that my creative brain stems from the same area of all the great writers!

I shall continue to weave my web like a spider in order to prove to Tessa and Simon that I can write. Richard was the only one who gave me any encouragement. He kindly bought me many boxes of good quality paper so that I could write my story. Poor Richard was in financial difficulties with his restaurant and I was going to help him recover his losses. We had this last hope that my book would eventually bale him out.

My web has broken several times and gone up in flames but I am prepared to try one more time. I shall stop writing to relax my brain because I want to watch 'The Booker Prize' on BBC2, besides tomorrow is another day.

Spiders have eight legs to help them spin their beautiful webs whereas I only have two which are getting very weak, but I can still walk. Some people have no legs, others have no arms and I am very lucky because at the moment I can still use my hands but I have aches and pains in all my joints starting from my head to my toes and writing can become very tiring.

Ode to Terrorists

I began rewriting *Odes To Toads* after having my letter to the editor on terrorists published in the *Surrey Herald*. The letter reads as follows:

Pen is mightiest
You will find that men are mainly terrorists. Little boys play with guns from an early age and little girls with dolls. I was once a little girl and I thought that this great big, beautiful world was full of good people, but now at the age of 78 I have come to realise it is full of terrorists.

Anyone who performs an act of violence against another human being or an animal is a terrorist. To quote the Bible, an eye for an eye and a tooth for a tooth is wrong because we have all forgotten that we must learn to turn the other cheek.

'The news is full of the horror terrorists have caused in New York but if we all go to war for this unbelievable disaster we will regret it.

The only way to save ourselves and our planet is to use the art of communication. The internet can bring us peace on earth forever.

We have the gift of language. We may not all speak the same language but, fortunately, English is universally spoken throughout the world. I feel that Great Britain, which is now my home, must set a good example to the world by agreeing only to have a war of words.

I was brought up in romantic India and I saw the horror of The Great Calcutta Killing, which will remain in my memory forever.

My ancestors were Portuguese, Spanish, English, Irish and a sprinkling of Dutch.

I am very proud of the fact that I have many nationalities in me but most of all we must not forget that we are all human beings. None of us are going to live forever, so why fight with one another?

Death is our common enemy because it is the biggest terrorist of all and in my eyes war is mass murder.

We need a war of words in order to be able to communicate with one another until all the terrorists are found, tried and justly

punished.
The pen is mightier than the sword.

Ode to Letters from my Foreign Children

I got a letter from Cesar this morning, acknowledging the letter I sent to the Editor of the *Surrey Herald*. Cesar is Spanish, he is a banker and his letter is very meaningful.

The handmade card from Oliver captures his delightful personality. Oliver was French, he was twenty-one years old and he was a typical young Parisian full of charm! He lodged with me for four months this year.

Lynda's letter is intelligent. She was a friend's au pair, she did my housework once a week. She had a lovely eccentric character. She was eighteen years old and very attractive.

I normally file all my foreign guest's letters but when the file becomes too full I sort out my special favourite friends and destroy the rest. I keep my whole life in files in a very useful mahogany cabinet in my drawing room. I have an open plan drawing room cum dining room with an open plan kitchen. As one can imagine I have to be a very tidy person, especially when I am writing a book. I sit at my dining table in front of a lovely antique clock which keeps on repeating tick, tock, tick, tock, tick, tock.

This friendly clock constantly reminds me that 'TIME' which is so precious is marching on.

X 2001

Dear Mrs Rumsey
I received your letter, published by the Herald, 'the pen is mightiest than the sword'.
You have always been a wonderful writer and better talker as a human being. But nowadays writing is being manipulated, talking is difficult and we don't know what is being human person.
Terrorism is very old. It appears when men not only are

157

incapable of communication, but when our system becomes obsolete; it needs renovation. We only are capable of increasing material welfare, and not enough. People demand more and more of 'something else' which has to be with your communication, but in a higher level; a more human level; what we have always searched in between our actual mediocrity; what you call 'communication; with big letters; and, as always anywhere, we need a mightier pen. That is the endless problem. Perhaps it is in the essence of world.

Autumn is coming and I remember the end of my summers in England with your family. The walks and talks with you trying to develop my English and my life. I did not feel far away from my country, but near other ones. You made me feel in that communicative state, although my pen was not still enough advanced. Now I can remember with pleasure and I understand that you have always been an extraordinary writer, full of art and capable of imagination and reflecting life.

Now you revolt yourself against terrorism because you know and understand it by yourself. You know what makes this world cry and what can arrange it. You have suffered it in yourself and have fought against it with the pen of your heart.

04.10.01

Dear Bridget
I have receive yesterday the Herald dated Sept 27, 2001 !!!
It was a great excitement first of all to receive this newspaper: What is inside??
<u>*Congratulation*</u>
And many thanks for such beautiful words.
It's a marvellous letter and such a right message
Thank you very much to write so beautiful think and to show your thought.
I hope you are all right and that I will see you very soon.
I am looking forward to see you and to read you.
Lots of love
Oliver

I do have a job proposition to go Richard (Saudi Arabia)

21 October 2001

Dear Granny,

Many thanks for your letter and I am so, so happy that you are getting better. I am fine now; but I am very busy in a school. I decided to learn Spanish and I have lots of work in university as well. And yes, I am going to be a lawyer. In Slovadie we have different school system and when we finished a high school, we have to study for 5 years if you want to be a lawyer. And I am studying for the 4th year now. And thanks for the newspaper, it's really great. Your letter in a paper is great; marvellous and I agree with you, but…you have to know, I don't agree with a war; with a violent way out… your letter is for intelligent people which understand what it means – life. A man, who decided to finish his life in a plane; for this man is life nothing. We can't use a communication, because they don't want to communicate, the only sense of their life is war. They can't think that they might do everything what they want to; because they will want more and more. The people are afraid to sit down in a plane, afraid to open an envelope and I think we have to protect our freedom. They can't think that they are the kings of the world. A man who have his gun in a bed can't understand our opinion, he doesn't care about our future. And, we communicated, we get them a choice, Ladin or war. And they choose their sense of life, this, what they love and now is our turn. Granny, just think of this disaster if we let Hitler to finish his terrible ideas and plans.

Lots of love, Granny,
Linda

Ode to my Birthday

I had my first birthday wish from Simon this morning at 9 a.m. from Anjou, in the Loire valley in France.

'The weather is perfect, warm with bright sunshine,' he told me. 'The clocks went back last night but the weather did not. As usual it is overcast, threatening to rain with odd glimpses of sunshine,' I remarked. Thomas, my six-year-old grandson sounded very grown up on the phone, one day he will be a perfect Anglo/French gentleman! Alexander was himself, he is only four so he forgot to wish me. He did let the cat out of the bag,

'We have presents,' he said.

'But it is my birthday,' I said.

'The presents are for two grannies,' he told me then he added, 'Happy Birthday.'

Last of all Nathalie, my French daughter-in-law, came on the phone.

'Happy Birthday Gran,' she said in her delightful French accent and the tears rolled down, 'Thank you Nathalie,' I replied, choking with emotion. 'I hope to see you on Tuesday with the boys,' I told her but she repeated, 'Have a good day today and enjoy yourself.' She did not promise to pop in on Tuesday but it is all my fault. I had a private disagreement with Nathalie a few months ago, which is our affair, but I hope she will forgive and forget it now because I like her. I like both Simon's wives, but I feel they should appreciate him more. They have had life easy with 'au pairs'. Poor Tessa only had an 'au pair' for a few weeks when she had a new baby.

The second person to wish me was June.

'Who's speaking?' I asked, not recognising her voice.

'It's June,' she said.

'Well I expect you to sing for me,' I told her jokingly and she burst into song. June and Julie have beautiful voices. My eldest sister Mary wished me last night. 'Aren't you going to sing for me Mary?' I asked playfully.

Her pretty voice sounded frail because Mary is eighty-four years old now but I recognised it.

My birthday luncheon party was held at 'The White House.' Tessa and Gerald had returned from Tunisia so Tessa did appreciate not having to cook. Angie did the catering and Maureen did the waiting. It was like being in India again.

Champagne was served with canapés – baby tartlets filled with prawns/smoked salmon and a dip with vegetable crudities.

Main course:

Roast sirloin of Scotch beef – horseradish/mustard,
Yorkshire puddings/red wine gravy

Medley of roasted vegetables:
carrots/broccoli/roast potatoes

Desserts:

Plum and almond crumble – fresh vanilla custard

Apricot d'acquoise – mango coulis

Lastly:

Cheese/crackers/grapes and coffee

Gerald put on a tape of Julio Iglesias at my request, because he is one of my favourite singers and the beautiful house took on a South American atmosphere. I opened my presents in the drawing room. Tessa and Gerald gave me two lovely pullovers. Simon gave me six exquisite crystal cut glasses. James gave me a box of Black Magic chocolates and a delightful jewel box.

Sophie bought me five sheets of beautiful handmade writing paper with envelopes to match, which was made in India, and bath salts. Lucy gave me a very unusual photograph album which had a rich purple and gold cloth cover.

Kate gave me a delicious box of stuffed dates from Tunisia and Emma gave me an exquisite glass perfume bottle. Dominic and Jessica also gave me a beautiful little perfume bottle. It is quite obvious from my collection of perfume bottles that my grandchildren know I love perfume!

Simon's handsome seventeen-year-old son Dominic and his exotic fourteen-year-old sister Jessica joined us for lunch, so we were ten people in all. The conversation during lunch was very stimulating and I found it was difficult to keep up with the children. It was a great pity that Simon and Nathalie and their two boys were not present. Simon's eldest son Oliver also could not make it because he was at his university in Exeter. It was a wonderful family gathering and we all enjoyed ourselves and the good food enormously.

All the youngsters, including Gerald, went for a drive after lunch and Tessa and I watched the TV. We had tea and birthday cake which was made by Sophie. It was one of my happiest birthdays but I had to spoil it all in the end because the tears flowed like rivers. The emotion was too much for me because I wanted Richard to be by my side – death is so final!

I am having a busy time at the moment because Julie and I do something different every day. We went to a bazaar which was held at Weybridge Hall in aid of St Christopher's Hospice and we bought one another parting gifts. Julie bought me a beautiful garnet and amethyst necklace and I bought her a bracelet. We have been friends for many years and at our age we may never meet again so I want this holiday to be a happy one.

I also bought two hand-embroidered little cushions, with beautiful words, 'Daughters are for ever I am glad you are mine' and 'A son brings joy that lasts for ever.' I have given Tessa her cushion and I told her I have only loaned her to Gerald.

I shall give Simon his cushion when he calls today with the children for tea. Simon visits me once a fortnight now.

It is a coincidence but I have come to realise I have an 'international' circle of friends. My car is cleaned by Bulgarians at Weybridge car park, inside and out for only £9.50. My hair is cut by an Italian and my dentist has an oriental name! Fi is my young Asian girlfriend and Agnes is a Hungarian girl who does my housework. My American girlfriend Judy and her delightful little girl, Amy, called to see me today and we took Julie with us to Garsons Farm for lunch.

I think we do not realise that Great Britain has become an International Island! Perhaps one day we shall be as prosperous as America? But I want to keep our Royal Family, just to be different. I am very much a Royalist at heart. Our National Anthem must also be sung and 'Land of Hope and Glory.' This meaningful song reminds me of Nazareth Convent boarding school in the Nilgri Hills in India. It was our end of term song.

Ode to the Past and Future

The happy days when I took lively students are in the distant past. Cesar visited me a couple of times in 'Noirmont Place' when he came to London on business. Tessa and I also visited Cesar once in Madrid because I wanted to give him *The Summer of my love*. I wrote this book when I took a course of Oestrogen.

It was a romantic story about a young man in the spring of his life and an older woman who was in the summer of hers. It was a beautiful story about romantic love.

I am looking forward to Friday, 28 December when I will meet Mr Charles Petters who will tell me more about my husband's secret life in Hampstead. Why this man should turn up at the end of my book may have to remain a mystery.

In my opinion it is the end, or the beginning of the end, or the end of the beginning of my writing career. I have got a lot of living to do!

These unusual odes have been written by a grandmother for grandmothers. Sadly I am a widow now and I hope all lonely widows will sit back and enjoy my stories as well. I want all OAPs who are only old children to think back on the days when they were young! Try to remember the song 'You make me feel so young!'

In conclusion I want to recall what a fortune-teller told Richard when we were boarding a ship at Bombay with our two children leaving India for the last time.

'Sahib,' he said, 'you are taking away a pearl from the Orient; one day the memsahib is going to make you a very rich man.'

Richard laughed but I put a silver rupee into this wise man's hands.

'Don't laugh, Sahib, I swear it will come to pass,' and I sincerely hope it does.

Ode to If
(Anonymous)

If you think you are beaten, you are
If you think you dare not, you don't
If you'd like to win, but think you can't
It's almost certain you won't.
If you think you'll lose, you've lost
For out of the world we find
Success begins with a fellow's will
It's all in the state of mind.
If you think you're outclassed, you are
You've got to think high to rise
You've got to be sure of yourself before
You can ever win a prize.
Life's battles don't always go
To the stronger or faster man
But sooner or later the man who wins
Is the one who thinks he can.

P.S. I remember once being told by a teacher when I was a little girl 'If, stands stiff in the corner.' I was always being put in a corner in the classroom for reciting my odes.

Richard's Cartoons

"OBVIOUSLY NOTHING WRONG WITH HIM——LET'S START RE-ASSEMBLING"

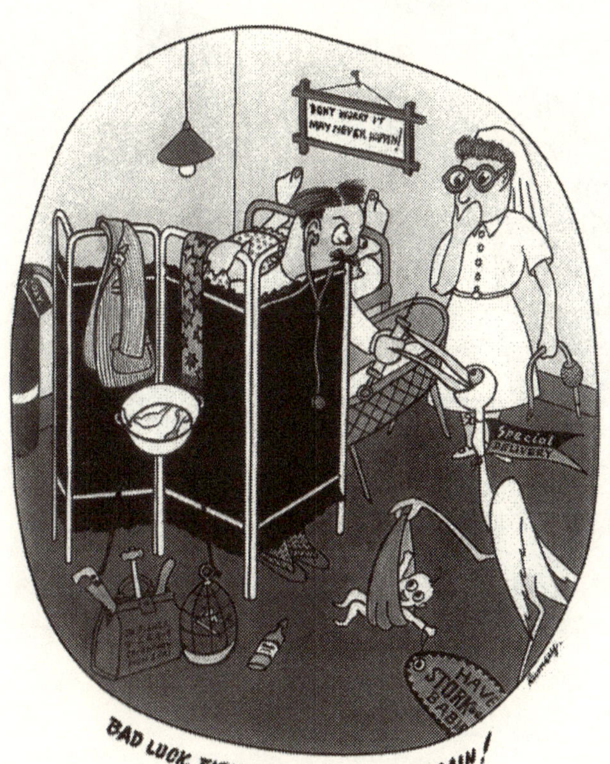

BAD LUCK FISH—BEATEN YOU TO IT AGAIN!

Getting to the Theatre on time!

My final Ode

I would like to thank my father's spirit for giving me the inspiration and courage to write *Odes to Toads*.

I want to thank Sharon Buroni for typing my manuscript and for her support and encouragement.

I also want to thank Diana Smith, Geraint Smith, Patrick Smith and Vanessa Long from Sunflower Graphics Oatlands for all their help in preparation of this book.

Last, but not least I want to say a big thank you to my South African lodger Robyn Woods for her prayers!

I feel like a Christmas cracker about to go off with a bang!

> At seventy-eight,
> I am getting late,
> For the Pearly gate,
> I have achieved my goal,
> May God rest my soul.'